For William Hurlbut,

with greetings from
St. Helena and the
author's compliments
and best wishes.

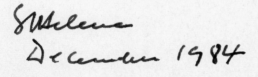

St Helena
December 1984

NAPOLEON'S LAST JOURNEY

❋   ❋   ❋

Gilbert Martineau

Translated from the French
by Frances Partridge

JOHN MURRAY

© Gilbert Martineau 1976
This translation
© John Murray (Publishers) Ltd 1976

Printed in Great Britain by
Cox & Wyman Ltd, London, Fakenham and Reading
0 7195 3293 0

To the Memory of
Dame Mabel Brookes
In token of a long friendship

Come, let's talk about the Emperor a little, it will do us good.

VICTOR HUGO

... but France shall feel the want
Of this last consolation, though so scant;
Her honour, fame and faith demand his bones
To rear above a pyramid of thrones.

LORD BYRON

It shone (his life) with a brilliance that the world had never seen before and will doubtless never see again.

GOETHE

History is his true country, it is there that he hopes to find the only rest suitable to him — to sleep in the stone of monuments raised to his glory.

FRIEDRICH SIEBURG

Napoleon was not made of the wood monarchs are made of, but of the marble gods are made of.

HEINRICH HEINE

A mortal man beyond all mortal praise.

W. S. LANDOR

CONTENTS

✱

CONTENTS

ILLUSTRATIONS

❋

*Reproduced from a book of lithographs by Victor Adam depicting the return
to France of Napoleon's body, published in 1840.

ILLUSTRATIONS

I

AFTER THE EMPEROR'S DEATH

❈

On July 25, 1821, the *Camel*, an old store-ship from the East, arrived 'some 160 leagues from the French coast' at the same latitude as Paris, with Napoleon's suite from St. Helena on board, whereupon General de Montholon proceeded to open the Emperor's will and read it aloud to the other executors, General Bertrand and Louis Marchand, in the presence of the Abbé Vignali.* Sometimes his voice was drowned by the coming and going of sailors on deck or the creaking of the timbers, sometimes by the murmur of the waves and the wind whistling in the rigging:

'I bequeathe ... I wish ... I appoint.'

Tristan de Montholon read slowly, deciphering the almost illegible handwriting with difficulty, and his words brought the past to life. With eyes closed, Bertrand and Marchand seemed to see all the ghosts of those epic days pass before them – La Valette, Drouot, Cambronne, Mouton-Duvernet, La Bédoyère, Brayer, Lefebvre-Desnouette, and even Hébert, the caretaker at Rambouillet, and Lavigne and Derrieux, Napoleon's grooms in Egypt. No one had been forgotten!

If Marchand had every right to exult as he remembered his master's flattering phrase ('he tended me with the kindness of a friend'), and to dream of projects made possible by the generosity heaped upon him, things were very different for poor Bertrand, Grand Marshal of the palace in exile, who was meagrely rewarded

* Chaplain at Longwood. He was the bearer of a copy of the will, given him by Napoleon himself and sealed under the secrecy of the confessional.

with a bequest of 500,000 francs, whereas Montholon pocketed 2 millions.

On July 31 at midnight, the *Camel* dropped anchor in Spithead roads, and on the morning of August 1 she fired twenty-one guns to salute the royal yacht, with the recently crowned George IV on board, about to leave for a visit to Ireland: meanwhile a boat appeared at the gangway, and Sir William Kepper of His Majesty's Household came on board to inquire after the health of the French officers and the Comtesse Bertrand.* Less than three months had passed since Napoleon's death, and everyone from the King's representative to the port officers avidly questioned these phantoms from the past who had received his last wishes after sharing his exile; for the prisoner's death, announced in the papers on July 4, was a universal subject of conversation and revived many old memories. Thus the French learned that the tone of the English reaction had been largely inspired by Sir James Mackintosh, an important figure in the world of politics and letters.†

'What a sensation this event would have made nine years ago and what a sensation it will make nine hundred years hence.'

For this philosopher and historian, 'of all great conquerors Napoleon is the most remarkable', and Sir Hudson Lowe's conduct on St. Helena was 'blameworthy'. This view was not shared by the East India Company, one of whose directors had declared bluntly, at a meeting:

'Then, Mr. Chairman, I congratulate you and the company!'

One of his colleagues bounded furiously to his feet:

'It is unmanly and ungenerous to rejoice at the natural death of one who has long been politically dead!'

The churlish director changed colour and explained pathetically

---

* The Prince of Wales had succeeded to the mad King George III on January 18. He had been Regent since 1811.

† Sir James Mackintosh (1765–1832), historian, philosopher, doctor of medicine, barrister, M.P., and a high official in the Indian Civil Service; he was author of a History of England and *Vindiciae Gallicae*, reflections on the French Revolution.

that he was merely rejoicing 'to see an end to the expenses of keeping up the establishment at St. Helena'.

'Fie!' was one gentleman's comment; meanwhile, at his club, the Duke of Wellington had publicly expressed his great admiration for Napoleon. Someone who did not hide his astonishment at this attitude was the chargé d'affaires to the King of France, the Comte de Caraman, who wrote in his report to his Minister: 'The special interest aroused by extraordinary destinies seems to have been awakened by the certain news of Napoleon's death. His most constant and outspoken enemies have seemed struck as if by a remarkable event, and those who always took his part have not concealed their sorrow.' Three days later he added the scandalised note that certain Britons, Sir Robert Wilson for one, had gone into mourning in response to a placard appearing on London walls, appealing to all those who admired talent and courage in adversity to honour 'this premature death'.*

Such splendid enthusiasm on the part of an erstwhile enemy, was in marked contrast with the persecution and scorn of Sir Hudson Lowe and his clique, and the ghosts from St. Helena, authorised to disembark according to the simple regulations of the Alien Bill, were aware of the deferential interest they aroused at Portsmouth, where – according to Marchand – 'the population was curious to see men who had remained faithful in misfortune', and where the usually fussy customs officials exerted themselves to facilitate the passage of the conqueror's relics – silver, legacies and uniforms.

Bertrand and Montholon took rooms in London, in Brunet's Hotel, Leicester Square, and were at once treated as distinguished visitors, nor was their drawing-room ever empty. 'Bertrand is a small, plain-looking man, with lively eyes, but a mild expression, and mild manner, not so French as most Frenchmen,' notes

* General Sir Robert Wilson (1777–1849) formerly one of Napoleon's bitterest enemies, had been outraged by the persecution of the Bonapartists by the royalists and had sympathised with the escape of La Valette, Napoleon's Postmaster-General, during the Hundred Days, which had cost him three months in Louis XVIII's dungeons.

Hobhouse.* 'The Countess ill with a cough – a pale, tall, thin agreeable-looking woman of a certain age; the Count very solicitous about her health.' They were deluged in questions.

I asked him if it was true that he had shaken hands with Sir Hudson Lowe?

He answered: 'Que voulez-vous?' 'All was over: the Emperor was dead.'

'He says you were satisfied with his conduct.'

'Oh,' replied he, 'he always said so!'

On August 18, the executors of the will tackled the Longwood accounts, from the funeral expenses to gratuities to the soldiers who carried the coffin; from the return journey to Florence of Dr. Antommarchi, Napoleon's last doctor, to the cost of the second codicil.† The Emperor's privy purse, 'that nest-egg for a rainy day' brought out of France in 1815, had not proved sufficient even when increased by the Toilet account in Marchand's charge, and each of the three men had to produce a substantial advance. What incredible difficulties in winding up the affairs of a man who had slept above cellars full of gold at the Tuileries!‡

Each of them was burning to get back to his native land and his family, and their joy was great when on August 16 the French embassy provided them with passports stamped with the King's arms. There was a somewhat unpleasant moment when a policeman appeared and tried to seize the casts of the Emperor's death-mask, acting on the instructions of Dr. Burton who had made the original, but the attempt collapsed and their fears vanished. The Bertrands maintained that the mask itself belonged

---

* John Cam Hobhouse, Lord Broughton (1786–1869), writer and politician, Byron's friend from childhood. When Napoleon was at St. Helena he sent him his book on life in France during the Hundred Days with an admiring dedication. This so much annoyed Lowe that he appropriated the gift.

† The French had paid all the expenses of the funeral: Lowe only provided the quadruple coffin.

‡ There was only 301,330 francs in the privy purse and 26,503.20 francs in the Toilet account. Bertrand, Montholon and Marchand each had to find 13,644.50 francs.

to the Imperial Family and that the doctor must be content with a copy. Antommarchi stated that he was offered £6,000 for one of the two casts he made while he was in London. So that at this time there were three examples of the mask in existence: the original and two casts, one of which Bertrand deposited in a safe place in London.*

Marchand set off for Paris on the 19th, but Bertrand and Montholon remained in London so as to make the first official move towards having Napoleon's body returned to France, in the form of a request to the King of England through the Prime Minister, Lord Liverpool. 'We are fulfilling a religious duty imposed on us by the Emperor Napoleon's last wishes. We claim his ashes. Your ministers, Sire, know that it was his desire to lie amidst the people he loved so much. His testamentary wishes were communicated to the governor of St. Helena, but this official paid no attention to our requests, and had him buried in the land of his exile. Prompted only by her grief, his mother implores you, Sire; she begs you to return her son's ashes to her, she asks for the slight consolation of watering his tomb with her tears. If he ruled the world from his throne, and could still terrify his enemies from his isolated rock, now that he is dead only his glory can survive him.'

The reply was slow in coming, and it was only in December 1821 that they learnt from the lips of His Britannic Majesty's ambassador in Paris that the 'English government regarded itself as the trustees of the ashes, and that they would relinquish them as soon as the French government signified their desire for them'.

To tell the truth, the royalist government seemed far from eager to bring back to France the still warm remains of the Ogre, particularly as the news of the death agony at St. Helena had created very little stir, thanks to the complicity of the royalist press. The Court displayed a sort of relief, and it was left to Louis XVIII to adopt an amiable tone when speaking of the event, so as

---

* It is difficult to settle the question definitely, but there were probably the Malmaison mask (which would be the original) and two casts belonging to Bertrand and King Joseph – these last now in the collection of Prince Napoleon.

to pacify the Bonapartists. General Rapp, first chamberlain, shed a few tears and apologised for his weakness.*

'I was "his" aide-de-camp for fifteen years, and I'm not ungrateful.'

'Rapp, I know you are very distressed by the news I've received,' said the King graciously. 'It does honour to your feelings; I like and esteem you the better for it.'

These august words, reported by the *Journal des Débats*, set the tone, and the court decided on grief to order. Only Talleyrand, always miserly with his feelings but prodigal with his epigrams, was ungenerous towards the man he had admired, served and betrayed for so many years. A lady gave him his opportunity.

'Oh, good heavens, what an event!'

'It's not an event any more, it's news,' he murmured.

The press was laconic, sometimes sarcastic. For one news-sheet like *Le Constitutionnel*, which announced without beating about the bush: 'We need not be afraid to say that the prisoner at St. Helena will be counted among the great men of the world', there were many to accuse the Emperor of 'not having made a good death', or to proclaim that he had met his end a 'forgotten' man. 'His natural death' suggested *La Foudre* on July 20, 1821 'was just a news item like any other. It was talked about for two or three days, like rain or fine weather. Now no one thinks about it.' *Le Journal des Débats* showed more style and stated: 'We have felt diffident about hastening to express our personal feelings for this extraordinary man, solely out of fear of seeming to distort the truth either through hatred or false generosity;' but *Le Journal du Commerce* only got out of the difficulty by an amphigory: 'It is not always death that ends the lives of great men,

---

* Jean Rapp (1771–1821) aide-de-camp to Desaix and then to Bonaparte; after the Polish and Prussian campaigns he was made governor of Dantzig. He received his twenty-second wound at Moscow. In January 1814 he was taken prisoner by the Russians during the siege of Dantzig, went over to Louis XVIII, and again served under Napoleon during the Hundred Days. After Waterloo he was rewarded by the royal favour and became first chamberlain and Master of the Wardrobe.

Letizia, Madame Mère, in her old age,
drawn by her granddaughter Charlotte

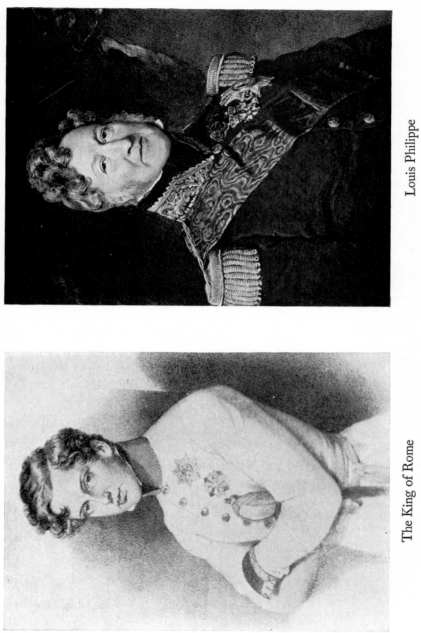

Louis Philippe

The King of Rome

and long before May 5, 1821, Napoleon's fate had been sealed on the field of Waterloo. But posterity has not yet given its verdict, and we doubt whether the hour of justice has even yet sounded.'

On the other hand, all those who had remained faithful, whether members of the old Imperial court or the army, displayed their grief and their mourning. Castellane, a veteran of the Russian campaign – who had been attached to the suite of the Duchesse d'Angoulême in 1821 before becoming Maréchal de France under Napoleon III – wrote in his *Journal*: 'The Emperor Napoleon belongs to posterity; he is now a great man, and no one dares dispute that title.' Colonel Fantin des Odoards said trenchantly: 'The nineteenth century will be Napoleon's century,' and another officer of the Empire, Commandant Persat, confessed 'I loved the Emperor as a son loves his father, and shall mourn him as such.' Planat de la Faye, who had been preparing to relieve Montholon at Longwood, was sunk in grief: 'Everything is over for me, I have lost everything that gave me strength, that gave value to my existence . . . I am like a man flayed alive; if anything touches me I yell; when people try to console me I fly into a rage.'*

The salons of the monarchists, for their part, were filled with a chorus of condemnation of the Usurper. The Comtesse de Boigne† mocked delightedly: 'I heard the street-criers calling: "Death of Napoleon Bonaparte for two sous; his speech to General Bertrand for two sous" – and it created no more stir in the streets than the announcement of a lost dog.' An English observer noted with consternation that 'the news of the death of the Emperor of Madagascar would not have been received with

---

* Louis Planat de la Faye (1784–1864). Aide-de-camp to Napoleon during the Hundred Days, he was nearly chosen to go to St. Helena in place of Gourgaud, who carried off the nomination after a violent scene. Planat tried to join his master in 1815 but only received the permission of the British authorities in 1821: it was too late.

† Louise d'Osmond, Comtesse de Boigne (1781–1866), closely involved with Baron Pasquier, saw herself as a political Egeria. Her salon was all the rage in Louis Philippe's day. Her *Memoirs* are always amusing and witty, but seldom kind.

more indifference,' and Baron Pasquier, the Foreign Secretary, calmly assured the French Ambassador in London: 'We see from the English gazettes that this event has created more sensation in England than in France. The French, with their lively imaginations thought of his death as occurring at the moment when his political career ended, and so the news had made no impression.' This from a man called Pasquier! A man who owed everything or almost everything to the Empire, and who cheerfully ended one of his dispatches: 'With him a great many dreams, a great many ambitions and hopes ought to come to an end, which nothing had formerly discouraged.' Nothing, certainly, had discouraged the dreams and ambitions of an office-seeker under the Bourbons.

*   *   *

Such was the atmosphere when Marchand presented himself at the headquarters of the Paris police on August 30 to request a passport and visa to go to Auxerre where his family lived. His stay in Paris was brief, for he was in a hurry to return to his native Burgundy where he was eagerly awaited by his mother, who had been head nurse to the Roi de Rome when a baby, was christened *Chanchan* by the child, and dismissed in March 1816. Well provided for by the Emperor, he was soon to become a middle-class citizen living peacefully on his property 'Le Verger' at Perrigny, wisely keeping away from factions, and going seldom to Paris, usually for a consultation with the other executors of Napoleon's will. Napoleon had given him a diamond necklace that once belonged to Queen Hortense and was valued at 200,000 francs. Beside the bequests in the second codicil, he had received further amounts of 74,000 francs, and found himself the possessor of a little hoard which would amount to 248,572 according to the will and make him a rich man by 1826. (In 1825 he married Mathilde, daughter of General Brayer, peer of France during the Hundred Days. He lived partly in Paris, where he had rooms in the Place du Palais-Bourbon and partly in his villa at Trouville where he died in 1876, aged eighty-five, the last French survivor from St. Helena.)

The executors were surprised by their respectful reception in France: if Montholon was covered by the law of amnesty of June 1821, Bertrand was still under sentence imposed on him during his absence, and his safety depended only on royal magnanimity. That good-natured prince Louis XVIII advised him to apply to the Minister of Justice. This formality over, Bertrand's rank was restored to him and he retired to his estate in the Berri, making only short visits to Paris, to stay in the fine house in the Rue Chanreine he owed to the Emperor's munificence. Montholon went off to his château at Frémigny, where he lived in lavish style, making frequent excursions to the capital.

Antommarchi had returned to Italy where he was coldly received by the Imperial Family. He tried without success to get Marie-Louise to execute a dubious codicil which might well have been in Montholon's handwriting: 'I beg Marie-Louise to take into her service Antommarchi, to whom I bequeathe a pension for life of 6,000 francs, to be paid by her.' He was firmly shown the door by General Neipperg, now the lover and adviser of the ex-Empress.

Saint-Denis, librarian at Longwood, settled at Sens; Noverraz, the usher, in Switzerland; Pierron, the chef, at Fontainebleau; Archambault, the groom, at Sannois; and Chandelier, the chef, at Paris. The Abbé Buonavita, who shared the chaplainship of the exiles with Vignali, received a parish in Mauritius, where he died in 1833.

* * *

The news of the Emperor's death, known on July 4 in London and in Paris on July 5, had not yet reached Rome when Madame Mère received the Abbé Buonavita on the 11th; he had left Longwood on March 17, bringing an alarming letter about the health of the illustrious invalid from Montholon to the Princess

Pauline: 'He is extremely weak, he can barely stand the effort of half an hour's drive at a walking pace in his calash, nor can he even walk in his room without support . . . The Emperor counts on Your Highness to make known the true state of his illness to influential Englishmen. He is dying without succour on this dreadful rock. His sufferings are terrible.' Two months had passed since the prisoner for whom kings had been appealed to in vain had been lying beneath a nameless stone in Sane Valley, but Madame Mère once more refused to believe this cry for help: her brother and a German clairvoyant supported her in the illusion that her son had been miraculously transported away from St. Helena. Pauline lost her temper in her efforts to convince her, shed tears to persuade the old lady to take official steps, and finally induced her to write to Lord Liverpool and beg that the sick man should be moved: 'Surely British power can find means to keep him in a European climate, where he can recover his health with the help of a good climate, and consoled by the care of some member of his family? A desolate mother's heart should be eloquent enough, but I prefer to rely on your humanity and your good feelings.'

She sent a copy of this appeal to Lord Holland, an influential member of the Liberal party who had been opposed to the internment at St. Helena, at the same time calling down all the blessings of the recording angel on his head. She had also sought the testimony of Dr. O'Meara, who had been sent away from Longwood for having revealed the nature of the exile's malady. She had asked Lucien's and Jérôme's advice, and even overcame her repugnance sufficiently to appeal to the unfaithful wife: 'You know all that Napoleon has suffered . . . Use every means in your power . . . The chaplain, who has just been here, left him on March 17 lying on a sofa, talking of you and his son, and saying uncharacteristically that if they did not make haste to get him moved they would soon hear that his life had ended. May God preserve you, and if you still remember me, Napoleon's mother, accept the assurance of my affection.'

A week later, Cardinal Fesch brought the fatal news to the Rinuccini palace. After parting from her brother, Madame Mère took over this palace on a corner of the Piazza Venezia. Here she lived among the portraits and busts she had sent for from Paris after the sale of her mansion at Brienne to Louis XVIII's government. The mother of kings shut herself away with her memories: 'My life ended with that of my son,' she wrote later. 'From that day I renounced everything for ever.' She went into mourning for the rest of her life.

At Parma, embarrassment prevailed over grief when the Piedmont Gazette published a paragraph concocted by General Neipperg. Marie-Louise received the confirmation of her widowhood from the Austrian embassy in Paris and put up a conventional show of regret: 'Although I never had warm feelings of any sort for him, I cannot forget that he is the father of my son, and that far from ill-treating me, as the world believes, he always showed me every consideration, and that is all one can wish for in a political marriage ... While one must be glad that he ended his unhappy life as a Christian, I could have wished him many years more of happy life, so long as it was far from me.'* She also wrote to her confidante the Duchess of Montebello: 'I have been very much shaken and upset, for it would have been unfeeling not to remember that the dead man was always good to me during the short time I lived with him,' and to Madame de Crenneville: 'Although I was parted from my son's father, death effaces all grievances and is always a painful shock, especially when one thinks of his horrible sufferings of the last few years. I should be quite heartless therefore if I had not felt extremely moved by it.'

The Court went into mourning for three months on July 25, 'on the occasion of the death of His Serene Highness the husband of our august Sovereign, which took place on the island of St. Helena on May 5 last', and the ex-Empress directed that a thousand Masses be celebrated at Parma, and as many in Vienna. She was even present at the funeral service in the chapel of her villa,

* Letter to Madame de Colloredo.

but modestly swathed in black veils to conceal her condition, due to the fact that nine days later she gave birth to her second illegitimate child by Neipperg, the future Prince of Montenuovo. As Neipperg described the ceremony to Metternich: 'There was no emblem of any sort on the catafalque, nor any ornament which could have recalled the past.'

The orphan of Schoenbrunn, a pretty fair-haired child of ten, heard of his loss from the lips of his tutor, who had chosen 'the calm of evening' to impart it. He wept bitterly for the death of a father whose face he could hardly remember, but whose mysterious presence haunted his memories of childhood. His tears flowed more freely still when his mother's letter was read to him: 'I am quite sure that your sorrow is as deep as mine, for it would be ungrateful in you not to remember all his kindnesses to you in your early years. You must try and imitate his virtues, while avoiding the reefs which strewed his course.'

At Vienna, Metternich prevailed over the Emperor Francis, who wanted the Court to go into mourning: only the household of the Duke of Reichstadt was authorised to conform to protocol. Marie-Louise was horrified to learn that Napoleon hoped that his heart would be sent to her . . . She begged her father to oppose the execution of this wish: she was afraid, she wrote, that Parma would become 'a place of pilgrimage'.

*   *   *

On August 15 the anniversary of Napoleon's birth, Madame Mère wrote to Lord Castlereagh, Foreign Secretary to the British government, to beg for her son's body, in a letter full of noble feeling: 'The mother of the Emperor Napoleon comes to plead that his enemies will return her son's ashes. . . . Even in remotest times, among the most barbarous races, hatred was not prolonged beyond the tomb . . . What pretext can be found for refusing to give up those immortal remains? Reasons of state or anything in the realm of politics have no concern with inanimate remains . . .

My son no longer has need of honours; his name is glory enough
. . . I implore His Britannic Majesty to grant me my son's remains;
I gave Napoleon to France and to the world. In the name of God,
in the name of all mothers, I come before you as a suppliant my
Lord, asking that my son's remains should not be refused me.'

The noble Lord did not reply.

With Napoleon dead, his family dispersed and under ferocious
supervision, and his supporters muzzled, the Courts of Europe
believed that that terrible spirit had been buried under the
tombstone at St. Helena. They counted without the poets and
without the common people – the true arbiters of fame – without
the painters and musicians, for whom the glory of a hero purified
by martyrdom was to provide an inexhaustible source of inspiration.

II
THE BIRTH OF THE LEGEND

*

'Brumaire 18 marked the beginning not of slavery, but of the enchantment of all minds,' Victor Hugo was to write in 1830, after revising his royalist opinions and tuning his lyre to the mood of the day, but ever since 1821 many writers had been basing their thoughts on the phrase which Stendhal was later to put into the mouth of Henri Brulard: 'My present esteem for Napoleon is engendered by the scorn inspired in me by all that has followed him.' The Emperor's capture by English ships and his exile 'across the sea' in an inaccessible and murderous island, were events designed to impress the popular imagination, and the legend, with the powerful backing of Hugo and Stendhal had begun to take shape by 1815. First, among the twenty thousand or so half-pay officers haunting the cafés of the Palais Royal and provincial bars, wearing long cloaks decorated with the ribbons of the Legion of Honour. These were the men who passed on rumours that the Emperor was at this moment in Isère, that he was going to reappear, that he was cruising off the coast of Corsica in preparation for a landing in the Midi, that he had escaped from St. Helena 'by an underground passage', or that he was awaiting his moment in Egypt . . . People took to seeing false Napoleons, such as one who visited an innkeeper of St. Paul-de-Varax in 1817 and cheerfully announced: 'I am the Emperor,' adding in front of the stupefied peasantry: 'Things will go a lot better when Napoleon II is king and I am his lieutenant-general.'

'His' proclamations were printed in clandestine news-sheets, and distributed on the marble tables of small taverns known as *goguettes*, and called *Les Lapins*, *Les Braillards*, *Les Vrais Français*, *Les Grognards* or *Les Amis de la Gloire*. They were frequented by workmen, artisans and old soldiers, who cheerfully squeezed up closer, like a family at home, to make room for new arrivals. At the *Enfants de la Gloire* or *Sacrifice d'Abraham*, they ate rabbit stew and, after a drink or two, burst out singing wildly:

> 'Il ne mit jamais sur sa tête
> Qu'un modeste petit chapeau
>
> Il fumait avec les soldats
> Et mangeait leurs pommes de terre.'

or else the popular songs of Debraux:

> 'Ah, qu'on est fier d'être Français
> Quand on regarde la Colonne
>
> Il reviendra le Petit Caporal
> Vive à jamais la redingote grise!
>
> Sur son rocher de Sainte-Hélène
> Honneur à la Patrie en cendres.'

In 1817 Charlet published his first works, recalling the glory of the armies of the Empire: *The grenadier of Waterloo*, *The death of the cuirassier*, *The defence of the flag*, *The French after the victory;* while Stendhal dedicated his *History of Italian painting* to Napoleon – at the same time, it is true, that he got the mayor of Grenoble to give him an affidavit proving that he had held no official position during the Hundred Days.*

In the same year a French translation of the *Letters of William Warden*, doctor on the *Northumberland*, was on sale in Brussels; it had been a success with the English public the year before, though it had little historical merit, but was rather a collection of anecdotes and witticisms, sometimes embellished and often garbled.

---

* Nicolas Charlet (1792–1845). Pupil of Gros, painter and lithographer, he held the same place in popular engraving as Béranger and Debraux did in song.

'It has a basis of truth,' grumbled Napoleon, 'but there are *cento coglionerie* and *cento bugie*.'

The serious *Edinburgh Review* judged it to be a publication of value however, because Napoleon's character was 'neither contaminated by adulation nor disfigured by coarseness in it'. Even at Longwood it had aroused controversy, and the Emperor, for lack of anything better to do, had set himself to refute this hollow book in a series of letters, which were translated by the Comtesse Bertrand and saw the light in London under the title of *Letters from the Cape of Good Hope in reply to Mr. Warden*.

To keep the faithful on the alert, the publisher John Murray also appositely launched a *Manuscript from St. Helena, written by an unknown hand*, attributed by some to Benjamin Constant, by others to Madame de Staël, whereas it was actually by the Swiss writer Lullin de Chateauvieux. Talleyrand, Marmont and Molé all thought it was from the pen of Napoleon himself: manuscript copies were made and circulated in drawing-rooms and cottages. At the same time an underground sale of souvenirs began, which are still to be seen today in the glass cases of museums or family cupboards: knob-sticks representing the Emperor's face, snuff-boxes or inkstands shaped like cocked hats, tricolour braces, and handkerchiefs embroidered with violets, miniature bronze busts in imitation of the column in the Place Vendôme. There was similar activity, arousing the suspicions of Louis XVIII's police, in the theatres, where the great names of the Empire still reigned supreme – Talma and Fleury, Mademoiselle George and Mademoiselle Mars. From March 22, 1817, the Comédie-Française put on Arnault's *Germanicus*,* whose author, 'a friend of Bonaparte's', was the bête noire of the ultras; the performance took place in a

---

* The extremists were angry with Arnault, for having composed a very neat epigram:

> 'Quoi qu'on pense, et qu'on puisse dire
> Le regne des Bourbons me cause de l'effroi
> J'ai vu le Roi; le pauvre Sire
> J'ai vu Monsieur . . . Vive le Roi.'

regular uproar with fisticuffs and fighting with sticks: the tragedy, inspired by Tacitus, was suspected of countless allusions to the problems of the day and shouts burst out:

'Down with the rabble!'

'Down with the Jacobins and the Bonapartists.'

'Down with informers!'

Royalists and old soldiers were thrown out, at the same time as young supporters of the new theatres; the play was banned, Talma denounced, and the legitimist newspapers asked in vain for him to be forced to retire. A lot of fuss about nothing, all things considered, since it was a bad tragedy and the verses smelt of the midnight oil, but the party in power saw the performance as a manifestation of Bonapartism, and openly blamed Louis XVIII for supporting an exiled writer.

Banned from the theatre, the opposition tried to mount a final attack for honour's sake, in the form of a spectacular revue, to the great delight of Alexandre Dumas who thought it amusing that 'Leipzig and Waterloo should be avenged on the battlefields of the Gymnase and the Variétés'. The affair again ended in the police station, and elegant audiences, delivered from these tiresome echoes of the past, could at last devote themselves again entirely to the works of the Vicomte d'Arlincourt, Ancelot's *Louis IX*, and Abrigny's *Jeanne d'Arc*, the customary fare provided by the Comédie-Française.

The opposition was powerless, and had to console itself with witticisms. When Wellington narrowly escaped a bullet fired by the ex-warrant-officer, Cantillon, the people of Paris sang:

> 'L'imbécile a visé trop haut,
> Il l'avait pris pour un grand homme.'

The bullet went through the Iron Duke's hat . . . Cantillon was bequeathed a legacy of 10,000 francs in Napoleon's will: 'He had as much right to assassinate that oligarch as the latter had to send me to die on the rock of St. Helena.'

But at the same time the English soldiers who were occupying the capital shouted insolently and effectively in the face of French veterans:

> 'Louis Dix-huite, Louis Dix-huite
> We have licked all your armies and sunk all your fleet.'

*　　*　　*

The censorship of the theatrical repertory and the press did not slow up the progress of the legend: it was in fact represented by the number of seat-holders at the Comédie-Française, a sale of 56,000 copies of a daily paper in a country containing about 50 per cent illiterates. . . .

The real propagandists were the colporteurs, with their heads full of the songs Paris was singing, and their placards decorated with even more subversive lithographs. Béranger was their favourite stock-in-trade: 'Perhaps at the present time I am the only author who can gain popularity without recourse to print,' he used often to say. Béranger, who had veered from dyed-in-the-wool liberalism to an odd sort of Bonapartism in the course of time . . . After 1818 in fact, and until 1820, the liberal opposition fell into step with the Bonapartists, less from deep conviction or desire to glorify Napoleon than from the need to use the legend of the triumphant Empire against the gloomy Bourbon régime, prostrated as it was by the after-effects of the war and the humiliating occupation.

Perhaps it was not such a bad thing, after all, that the Emperor's faithful followers and the defenders of the Republic should make common cause in a struggle against a retrograde monarchy, which could not forget that it was at the mercy of the Allies. Yet surely it was a curious idea to represent liberalism by a flag bearing the figure of a conqueror and authoritarian legislator . . . This audacity, however, produced unanimity among the troops, where ex-officers and officials of the Empire were in a majority, and eager to prove that their late sovereign had dreamed only of being 'the type and standard of liberal ideas', as the exile wrote from St. Helena with the pen of Las Cases.

The mouthpieces of this campaign were *La Bibliothèque Historique* and *La Minerve*: the first (escaping censorship by appearing at irregular intervals) was founded by a former collaborator of Maret, one of Napoleon's ministers, and a journalist on the *Nain Jaune*, 'journal of the anti-extinguishers'; the second opened its columns to all writers and journalists who frequented Arnault's during the Empire, along with a few select recruits such as Benjamin Constant and Béranger.* Béranger was a curious customer, anticlerical and autodidactic, former protégé of Lucien Bonaparte's: if Emile Debraux was the 'people's poet' and helped create the legend with his songs, Béranger was the favourite of the liberal middle-classes, of shopkeepers and artisans, and did not become the minstrel of Napoleonic glory until after 1830: when in 1818 Debraux published his *Ode to the Column* and found himself famous overnight, Béranger distilled less compromising couplets about the tricolour and the soldiers,

> 'qui se dérobant aux outrages
> Ont au ciel porté leur drapeau.'

or about the canteen-women,

> 'Si je vois de nos vieux guerriers
> Pâlis par la souffrance
> Qui n'ont plus, malgré leur lauriers
> De quoi boire à la France
> Je refleuris encore leur teint.'

There were few allusions to the man he always called 'the conqueror', but the public read between the lines, and when the song-writer turned his talents to verses in favour of a collection for the ex-officers who had taken refuge at the Champ d'Asile in the United States, or when his rhymes glorified the Old Flag, it

---

* It is impossible to analyse Béranger's work or assess his influence without referring to Jean Touchard's lively and rich thesis: *La gloire de Béranger*. (Armand Colin, 1968.)

was quite clearly the Emperor he was resuscitating, formidable and paternal:

'Un homme enfin sort de nos rangs.
Il dit: je suis le dieu du monde.'

In 1821, Napoleon's death authorised every sort of audacity, and Debraux composed the song he called *St. Helena:*

'Bon voyageur, verse des larmes
Ici mourût Napoléon.'

And in *How can we forget him?:*

'Non, non, jamais, tant que mon coeur battra
Ce nom chéri n'en disparaîtra.'

Meanwhile Béranger published *The 5th of May*, the song of a veteran, voyaging near the accursed rock in a Spanish ship, from which Berlioz made a cantata for 'solo bass, mixed choir and orchestra' in 1831.*

Pierre Lebrun, official poet under the Empire, was the writer of a lyric that cost him his pension, but it was Talma who created the biggest scandal of all, in December 1821, by his performance of Jouy's *Sylla.*† He came on to the stage so perfectly made up, with the lock of hair so well imitated and *his* gestures so carefully copied, that the audience felt a thrill of fear, and thought they were looking at Napoleon himself, as he said:

'Je me suis fait dictateur. Je sauvai la patrie. . . .
J'ai gouverné le monde, à mes ordres soumis
Et j'impose le silence à tous mes ennemis:
Leur haine ne saurait atteindre ma mémoire
J'ai mis entre eux et moi l'abîme de ma gloire.'

* The song *The Old Flag*, although dated 1820, appeared in the collection of 1821. To the tune of *She likes to laugh, she likes to drink*, an old soldier who has hidden a tricolour flag under his mattress, hums insolently:

'Viens mon drapeau, Viens mon espoir,
C'est à toi d'essuyer mes larmes.'

† *Sylla*, tragedy in five acts by the liberal writer Etienne de Jouy (1764–1846), first performed on December 27, 1821.

The outraged government resolved that an example must be made. In October Firmin-Didot had published 10,000 copies of Béranger's collected works: the author's name would be struck off the university staff – he had a modest office job there – the prosecutor would bring an action, and the work would be seized. He drew a blank because all copies of the book were already sold, and Dupin, the song-writer's barrister, teased gaily: 'The ten thousand are in retreat.'

These delayed persecutions did not take the editor unawares: realising that *The Old Flag* was audacious, he had taken the precaution of adding a note of explanation: 'This song only expresses the desire of a soldier to see the constitutional Charter placed in safety under the flag of Fleurus, Marengo and Auster-litz.' All was in vain, the whole collection of poems was under attack, as an outrage against public and religious morality, an offence against the King's person, and (in the case of *The Old Flag*), incitation of the public to demonstrations not authorised by law ... The song-writer was sentenced to three months imprisonment and 500 francs fine, but he looked on the bright side, thinking perhaps of the 30,000 or so francs he would earn from his collected poems, and admitted maliciously to a friend: 'I still have the esteem of good Frenchmen and myself.' The result exceeded his hopes: as the days passed peacefully at Sainte-Pélagie, he was showered with presents by his admirers and visited by pretty women and clever men, and became famous overnight.

At the same time a flood of often anonymous and always naïve couplets broke over the country with striking virulence. Whether it was *Sunset on the Fifth of May*, *A Tear on Napoleon's Tomb* or *Night at St. Helena*, the target was always England,

> 'Sois à jamais couvert d'une honte éternelle,
> Peuple anglais qui trahis sur ton sol infidèle
> Un guerrier malheureux,'

as Crébassol had already cried in his *Ode on the Death of Napoleon*. Fame also soon came to those who engraved the thousands of prints which decorated the houses of those who had not forgotten, and brought prosperity to those who sold them: Napoleon lying on his bed on the battlefield, surrounded by the soldiers of all his vassal nations, with the inscription: 'They aren't afraid now . . . Come close, all you conquered people, because if he wakes there'll be no more sleep for you'; or he would be standing in a familiar attitude, with: 'The transformation scene depicts Sesostris of Ancient Egypt, Caesar Emperor of Rome, Louis XIV King of France, Frederick King of Prussia and the East, all in person saluting with their laurels the shade of Napoleon, whom they are pleased to recognise as the man of genius who has surpassed them all.' Other themes glorified the Bertrand family, in tears by the tomb, and Horace Vernet worked at his painting of the *Grenadier at Waterloo*, though it was refused by the Salon of 1822.*

Police censorship kept an eye on these subversive activities, but could not prevent the peasantry assembling to hear the always embroidered tales of survivors, who tried to console themselves for half-pay or poverty by reviving the past, like Balzac's character in *Le Medecin de Campagne:*

'Come on, Monsieur Goguelot, tell us about the Emperor.'

The infantryman gets up and surveys the company with that dark gaze of his, overflowing with the misery, poverty, experience and sufferings typical of all old soldiers.

'Now listen carefully, and tell me whether what you hear is natural!'

'My children,' concluded a listener, 'he had to die, even *he*, but his memory – never.'

*   *   *

In 1822, one of the actors in the tragedy of St. Helena, Dr. O'Meara, doctor at Longwood from 1815 to 1818, threw his

---

* Horace Vernet (1789–1863), a fervent admirer of Napoleon. From 1807 to 1814 he painted heroic subjects, to which he returned in 1830 with his large pictures *Jena*, *Wagram* and *Friedland*. We also owe him a striking *Napoleon in Exile*.

Napoleon III

The Empress Eugénie on her visit to the tomb of
Napoleon on St. Helena

The opening of Napoleon's coffin on St. Helena

Napoleon in Exile or a voice from St. Helena in the face of the
British government; its evidence was sometimes mocking, sometimes sarcastic, but always implacable. The public devoured
with delight and anger mixed this account of conversations between Napoleon and his doctor, of quarrels with the sinister
gaoler, of the persecution of the defenceless exile, and the refutation by the Emperor himself of the crimes imputed to him by
English propaganda. In a few weeks the Irish Doctor had gained
celebrity and a fortune.*

Napoleon emerged from the book ennobled, even purified by
his end, but the gaoler of St. Helena, Sir Hudson Lowe, was
branded for ever as infamous by one of his own staff, and his
portrait hung in the rogues' gallery of history. Young Emmanuel
de Las Cases, intoxicated by the book, hurried to London to
join in the excitement; with his head still full of the trials of
exile, the vexations inflicted on his father, he twice struck Lowe
in the face in the middle of the street, and challenged him to a
duel, shouting to the passers-by who were about to manhandle
him:

'This man insulted my father.'†

Lowe had to flee before the outcry. He had left St. Helena in
July 1821, bringing with him the archives of his mission, and (in
his role as zealous collector) some of the Longwood furniture,
bought for a derisory sum – seven chairs, a chest of drawers, four
sofas, three mirrors, two book-shelves. For lack of space he had
to leave behind a writing-desk, which he specially wanted: 'It
was on this table,' he said, 'that Bonaparte wrote or got written
almost all the letters he sent me while he was in my charge.' In
his efforts to get hold of this precious piece of furniture in spite
of the opposition of his successor at St. Helena, he was involved

---

* Lord Byron devoted lines to him in *The Age of Bronze:*
　　'And the stiff surgeon, who maintained his cause
　　Hath lost his place, and gain'd the world's applause.'
† Emmanuel de Las Cases (1800–1854). Son of Napoleon's chamberlain in
exile. He was elected deputy after the July Revolution. Napoleon III made him a
Senator.

in a correspondence with the East India Company lasting five years ... He expected to be received in England as a person of consequence, although in fact he had many trials left to live through. He was foolish enough to bring an action against O'Meara, after intriguing to get the moral support of the Prime Minister and the Secretary of State for War, who quickly showed him the door. The Prime Minister, Lord Liverpool, had very little sympathy for this tiresome underling who revived the awkward past in such an embarrassing way, and whom he already planned to charge with responsibility for the harshness of Napoleon's detention. By the time he had completed his dossier, in 1823, the doctor's book was in its fifth edition, and the tribunal objected that the case was opening too late, and dismissed it. Lord Bathurst tried to console him by advising him to justify himself and write a history of his government of St. Helena: by concentrating on this, he might perhaps stop harassing the ministry with his complaints. He talked ceaselessly about the O'Meara affair, and wrote to the Prime Minister: 'Public curiosity flew with eagerness to the repast: nothing was wanting to satisfy the curiosity of the most credulous, the most inquisitive or the most malignant mind. The highest authorities are not spared, but I was destined to be the real victim, upon whom public indignation was to fall.' It was all no use, and instead of following this sensible advice, Lowe fussed around and increased his efforts to get a pension or a job. He was offered a sinecure – to govern Antigua, which he refused, and then to command the army in Ceylon, which he accepted. A few years later he was once more taken to task by a writer, but this time it was a national figure, the great Walter Scott himself, who alluded to his quick-tempered and irritable character, which had made him forget that his prisoner was in a position where he could not retaliate. He made a hurried return to London to defend himself. The Prime Minister, the Duke of Wellington, and Lord Bathurst (now President of the Council) explained to him in all seriousness that he had the chance of pocketing the post of governor of Ceylon if he would make sure of being on the spot when the vacancy arose, but at his farewell audience the conqueror of Waterloo did not mince matters: no firm promise as to the governorship and no pension, since Parliament would not vote such a measure 'as a reward for service at St. Helena', and the Home Secretary would be reluctant to propose it.* He could not have been more categorical, more brutal. When the post in Ceylon became vacant in 1830 the Liberals were in office, and as they had furiously attacked and condemned Lowe's treatment of Napoleon, he had to put paid to his hopes. He was sixty-one years old, lonely, with no job and full of bitterness. He returned to London to die, but his reputation was so unsavoury that his acquaintances avoided him. 'In five hundred years time,' his prisoner had predicted in 1816, 'Napoleon's name will shine over Europe, whereas yours and Castlereagh's will be known only for the shame and injustice of their conduct to me.'†

*   *   *

Another new book made even more of a sensation; it fulfilled a promise made in the courtyard of Fontainebleau after the first abdication, to some old soldiers who were in tears:

'I will write about the great things we've done together.'

Thanks to Lord Holland, Las Cases had got back the manuscript of his journal for 1815 and 1816, confiscated by Lowe, and towards the end of 1823 he published his *Mémorial* in eight volumes, which has so justly been described by Professor Dunan as 'a strange masterpiece of controlled enthusiasm'. It was

---

* His predecessor at St. Helena enjoyed a pension of £1,500 a year.

† Lord Castlereagh (1769–1822). Secretary of State for War and the Colonies in 1805, at the Foreign Office in 1812 and British representative at the Congress of Vienna; he was a furious enemy of Napoleon's. He cut his throat in a fit of madness, and Byron wrote an appalling epitaph to his memory:

'Posterity will ne'er survey
A nobler grave than this
Here lie the bones of Castlereagh,
Stop, traveller, and—.'

instantly recognised as the greatest literary success of the century.*
It was the bedside book of Stendhal's Julien Sorel, and when
Vigny wrote *Servitude et grandeur militaires* he studied it carefully
in search of the ardent schoolboy he had himself been under the
Empire, who used to interrupt Tacitus and Plato to shout 'Long
live the Emperor!'

That the little chamberlain, who had rallied to Napoleon rather
late in the day, it must be remembered, had tried above all to
produce a work of literature, that he sweetened certain passages to
avoid annoying the Restoration police – who, however, im-
prudently, had allowed the publication of this passionate apology
– that he sometimes exaggerated so as to please certain powerful
figures of the moment – that all these things helped gain him fame
must be conceded to his detractors; but he also deserves credit for
presenting the expectant public with a work of the greatest
nobility, for behind the puny silhouette of the author the formidable shadow of the Emperor can be clearly seen.

'The most charming thing about Napoleon,' wrote Stendhal,
'was his frankness, his good nature, his endless conversation
sparkling with wit, abounding in lively and picturesque images.'
All this was to be found in the *Mémorial*. In it one heard the
trenchant tones of a man who had governed and knew how to see
that he was obeyed, the disillusioned reflections of one who has
experienced desertion and treason, the melancholy of the builder
who sees his work unfinished, the attention to detail necessary for
a military commander, the boundless vision of a conqueror,
imperial anger and the simplicity of a sub-lieutenant. Old men
shed tears when they recognised the voice from beyond the grave,
and the young were inspired by the story of the exile's liberal
dreams, so different from those of the despot condemned by the
pamphleteers of 1815. What young lion could be unmoved by the

---

* Louis XVIII, who had published a little work called *The Journey to Coblentz*,
criticised the *Mémorial* harshly. 'M. de Buonaparte has published his memoirs
through the mediation of his chamberlain, Las Cases; I am happy to show him
that I can write my own myself.'

following apostrophe: 'Henceforth nothing can destroy or efface the great principles of our revolution. These great and beautiful truths must remain for ever, for we have laced them with gold and monuments, performed prodigies for their sake. Here is the tripod whence the light of the world will arise. These principles will constitute the faith, religion and morality of all races, and, whatever men may say, that memorable era will be connected with me in person, because after all it was I who lit the torch and consecrated the principles and now persecution has made me their Messiah ... Whatever equality is possible to give, has been given the French by me.' Here was material to inspire young men belonging like Vigny to the generation 'nourished by bulletins from the Emperor', as well as those who had returned their swords to the scabbards and begun to talk of the social struggle, and of emancipation and progress.

The wars with which Napoleon has so often been reproached were never undertaken except to guarantee national territory as defined by the Revolution, and to unify the peoples of Europe. 'The massing together of the Germans had to be slowed up, but I did no more than simplify their monstrous complication ... In any case, sooner or later, this massing together will happen in the natural course of events: the impulse has been given and I do not think that after my fall and the destruction of my system, any other European balance will be possible except the massing together and confederation of great nations.'

It must also be realised that the Consulate and the Empire were the fount of administrative order and social progress – striking proof that Napoleonic power had created a better society. 'My glory does not consist in having won forty battles ... but in my Code Civil ... in the reports of the Council of State.'

To pacify men's minds after the revolutionary storm, to reorganise the modern State, unify Europe, open careers to all talents – such was his achievement, or his dream. 'I have been an amalgamator, perhaps they will destroy me,' but what will then become of a continent divided 'according to colours and opinions?' Europe will either be 'Cossack or republican', under the covetous gaze of those two powerful giants America and Russia.

What a destiny, what glory and what plans for the child exiled in Vienna to inherit! And while Talleyrand's saying went the rounds of royalist salons: 'Well you see it's merely a question between the Duc de Bordeaux and the Duke of Reichstadt,' the dying Emperor's words took the form of a prophecy: 'I have implanted new ideas in France and in Europe, regression is impossible. My son must cultivate the seeds I have sown ... If he does he can still be a great sovereign. The Bourbons will not stay. After my death there will be a reaction in my favour everywhere, even in England. It's a fine inheritance for my son.'

*　　*　　*

In 1822 and 1823 two more books appeared – the *Mémoires de Napoleon*, dictated to, and brought back from St. Helena by Gourgaud and Montholon, and Arnault's *Napoléon*.* In 1824 came Ségur's *Histoire de Napoléon et de la Grande-Armée pendant l'année 1812*, with a proud dedication to the veterans of the Russian campaign: 'Where we are concerned with such a prodigious genius and such vast events, it seemed to me that nothing could be too detailed which helps us to understand to what lengths the endurance, glory and misfortunes of men can go.'† Gourgaud didn't find the book to his taste and criticised it so violently, describing the author as an 'armchair general', that the affair finished on the duelling-ground. In 1825 Antommarchi announced his *Les derniers moments de Napoléon*, an intolerably verbose outpouring, whose success was mainly due to curiosity. The last doctor at Longwood was short of cash; he had sold to a Comte Dzialinski manuscripts about Napoleon's youth, inherited

---

* After his return to France in March 1821, Gourgaud married the daughter of Roederer, former senator under the Empire, and although he lived in the country, assiduously frequented influential Bonapartists.

† The first two editions, of three and four thousand, were sold in a flash.

from St. Helena, though how they came into his possession was
not clear.

In 1827 Walter Scott published his *History of Napoleon
Bonaparte*, which pleased neither Lowe, who replied to the
criticisms of himself, nor Gourgaud, who also thought he had
been traduced. It was left to a young Rhinelander to take up the
cudgels against this 'blasphemy in twelve volumes' – the poet
Heinrich Heine, whose mind filled with 'images as gold and green
as spring' when he summoned up his memories of the Emperor of
Europe. 'An admirable thing, although the Emperor, the bane of
the English, is now dead and in his tomb, it is through him that
Britain's greatest poet has lost his laurels . . . The English merely
killed Napoleon, but Walter Scott sold him. It's a regular Highland fling.' At Dusseldorf one day, this German who was so happy
on the banks of the Seine, had been astounded to see Napoleon
riding in triumph through the Palace Gardens: the experience
marked him for life: 'My heart beat out the call to arms . . . The
astonished trees bowed down in time to his advance . . . The
Emperor leant casually forwards over his saddle, almost careless
of his seat; he held the reins high in one hand, with the other he
gave the little horse a friendly pat on the neck . . . It was a marble
hand, shining in the sunlight, a powerful hand, a hand which had
subdued anarchy – that thousand-headed monster – and ruled
over the conflict between nations.'

It was this Parisian Rhinelander who set the tone of admiration:
'The Emperor is dead. His lonely tomb stands on a little isle in the
Indian ocean, and HE, for whom the earth was too small, sleeps
peacefully under a miserable little hillock over which five weeping
willows despairingly trail their long green hair, and where a
pious rivulet trickles with a plaintive murmur. There is no
inscription to be seen on the tombstone; but Clio has engraved
there in invisible letters, words which will echo through the
remotest centuries.' These words make up the famous apostrophe
to England, the shame 'left behind by this illustrious man as
he died', his condemnation of 'the terrible hospitality of the

Bellerophon'. One day 'there will no longer be an England. That proud race will be lying in the dust . . . and St. Helena will be the Holy Sepulchre where the people of East and West will come on pilgrimages on ships decked with bunting.'

In London itself, another romantic poet, a proud and solitary genius was braving the thunder of Court and public opinion. Lord Byron, in revolt against his time, was writing in *The Age of Bronze*:

> 'Save the few fond friends and imaged face
> Of that fair boy his sire shall ne'er embrace,
> None stand by his low bed – though even the mind
> Be wavering, which long awed and awes mankind:
> Smile – for the fetter'd eagle breaks his chain,
> And higher worlds than this are his again'.

In 1827 *L'histoire générale de Napoléon* was announced – a sequel to *Mémoires sur le Consulat* by Thibaudeau, former president of the Convention and member of the Council of Five Hundred, as well as one of the authors of the Code Civil.

From the other side of the Rhine came Goethe's admission to Eckermann: 'It was *he*, and one only had to look at him to see that it was *he*.' For the romantic dramatist the Emperor was a 'demonic' being, an indomitable character, the equal of the Greek demi-gods. An octogenarian, and near his end, he read everything that was published about Napoleon, and deplored his harsh treatment at St. Helena. HE had no sheets on his bed. HE had to have his old suits turned. 'Isn't that an absolutely tragic touch?' One is reminded of Hegel, who was finishing his *Phenomenology of Mind* in 1806 when the French were besieging Jena, and who wrote to a friend: 'I've seen the Emperor – soul of the world – leave the town on a reconnaissance expedition; it is indeed a marvellous sensation to see such a man, sitting his horse at this concentrated point, and spreading his dominion over the whole world.' Goethe's interest was by no means isolated, and Chateaubriand notes at this same time in his *Mémoires d'Outre-Tombe*:

'Entering a village *en fête* in the Duchy of Baden, my hand was grasped by a drunk man who shouted "Long live the Emperor!" In Germany, everything that has happened since the fall of Napoleon is as if it had never been: these men, who took arms to preserve their national independence from Bonaparte's ambition are now dreaming only of him, so greatly has he stirred the imagination of all races, from the Bedouins in their tents to the Teutons in their huts.'

In 1828 Savary, the gendarme of the Empire, put his *Mémoires* before the public; the gesture was not without courage, because the royalists had never stopped attacking him over the affair of the Duc d'Enghien.*

The same year Béranger announced publication of a collection of songs in two volumes, the most famous being *Couplets on the battle of Waterloo*, *The Two Grenadiers* and *The people remember*, the last destined to become a popular song:

> 'Il avait petit chapeau
> Avec redingote grise
>
> On parlera de sa gloire
> sous les chaumes bien longtemps.
> L'humble toit dans cinquante ans
> Ne connaîtra plus d'autre histoire
>
> Parlez-nous de lui, grandmère.
> Grandmère, parlez-nous de lui.'

Béranger felt that the Napoleonic legend was a powerful ferment of national feeling and that it would attract and fascinate the popular classes; he let himself be carried along by the swelling tide all the more willingly because in December 1828 he was convicted of an offence against the person of Charles X and an outrage against the State religion, for publishing *The Coronation of*

---

* Savary, Duc de Rovigo (1774–1835). Aide-de-camp to Bonaparte, Napoleon's Minister of Police, inspector of the Gendarmerie during the Hundred Days. Having been unable to follow Napoleon to St. Helena, he was exiled from 1815 to 1819.

Charles the Simple and *Guardian Angel,* and was once more im-prisoned in La Force. He came out of prison with the text of *Quatorze juillet* in his pocket, soon to be sung in taverns, drawing-rooms and even in the Palais-Royal under the roof of the man who was to be King of the French two years later.

In 1829 Bignon embarked on a *History of France since the 18 Brumaire* in eleven volumes. He had entered the Foreign Service in 1797, and served the First Consul (later the Emperor) in Germany and Poland, and in recognition of his zeal Napoleon had left him 100,000 francs with instructions to 'write the history of French diplomacy from 1797 to 1815'. An embarrassing task, it must be said, for a man who had been sitting in Louis XVIII's Chamber of Deputies since 1817, but Bignon got out of this scrape diplomatically by declaring that having long served glory he now had the right to devote the rest of his life to liberty. Tired of examining official papers, he returned to his old faith, joined in attacking the English, was intoxicated by the accounts of imperial victories and ended by praising the political and social aims of the Empire . . .

In the same year Bourrienne, schoolfellow of the young Bonaparte and his secretary until 1802, but who later became an ardent royalist and swore fidelity to Charles X, undertook to collaborate with M. de Villemarest in compiling ten volumes of *Souvenirs,* overflowing with hatred for the leader he had cheated and deceived. There was an outcry among the faithful, who attacked both the spirit and the letter of the work, denying that Bourrienne had ever been in Bonaparte's confidence in Egypt, Italy or during the Consulate, emphasising improbabilities and boastfulness, as well as errors of names and dates. Nevertheless, as the author had lived in intimacy with his childhood friend during two long campaigns, he had seen a lot, listened hard and re-membered it all, and his chapters on every day life were as moving to the public as they were useful to historians. 'Bourrienne's memoirs,' wrote Stendhal, 'seem to me a piece of domestic treachery . . . Nothing could be flatter, more stupid than the aforesaid Bourrienne, but he has SEEN.' On St. Helena, Napoleon talked lightly about their intimacy. 'He corrupted the whole Household,' wrote Bertrand. 'He intrigued with Josephine and Hortense. Everything went through his hands. It was a fault in him ... At that time Talleyrand was partly on Bourrienne's side but he thought Bourrienne went too far, and warned him he'd ruin himself. "Oh no," said Bourrienne, "that's impossible. In Egypt I slept in the Emperor's tent." If Bourrienne had been a pretty boy, Talleyrand would have concluded that there had been a more intimate liaison.' Unhappy Bourrienne ... It was much too late to try and flatter a monarch whose throne was so rocky that old Talleyrand was declaring everywhere that 'he had brought back the Bourbons in 1814 for the sake of peace, but they would have to be thrown out again for the sake of peace in 1829'; and too late also to develop a taste for the pettiness of the Ultras, Charles X's retrograde absolutism and the vindictive arrogance of the Allies. The Austrian ambassador at Paris had received orders not to announce the marshals by the titles they acquired in the Empire, but by their names alone: the Duc de Dalmatie was now only the Marshal Soult and the Duchesse d'Istrie, Madame Bessières ... Charles X indignantly took the side of the marshals and Hugo published a vengeful ode:

> 'Je comprends, l'étranger, qui nous croit
> Sans memoire,
> Veut feuillet par feuillet déchirer
> Notre histoire
> Ecrite avec du sang à la pointe du fer.'

As for the new poetry, like politics it was coming to a cross-roads, nor was it any longer afraid to evoke the memory of *L'Autre* through the lips of Victor Hugo. This son of a general of the Empire and a Vendean mother had published his highly royalist *Odes et poésies diverses* in 1822; they had gained him a pension of 1,000 francs and the red ribbon, but five years later he was won over to liberalism, and had become obsessed by the

ambition to be the foremost lyric poet in France, as well as by the
superhuman element in Napoleon's character and his stupendous
achievements. It was impossible for him to be indifferent to such a
tumultuous genius, adventurer in ideas and manipulator of words.
Declaring that romanticism was 'liberalism in literature', the one-
time royalist nostalgically remembered his early childhood, and
the 'hero with the sweet smile'.

The preface to *Hernani* soon blazed into words which could
have been forged at St. Helena: 'In time of revolution, everything
moves forwards . . . In literature, as in society there is no etiquette,
no anarchy: only laws. Neither red heels, nor red caps.' This was
the literary programme of a century 'given its liberty by Mirabeau
and power by Napoleon'.

At the tomb of Charlemagne, Don Carlos was crying aloud to
all Paris:

> 'Ah! briguez donc l'Empire et voyez la poussière
> Que fait un empereur.'

And in 1828 Hugo dared present his publisher with the provocative poem he called *Lui*.

> 'Toujours lui! Lui partout! Ou brûlante ou glacée
> Son image sans cesse ébranle ma pensée.
> Il verse à mon esprit le souffle créateur.
> Je tremble, et dans ma bouche abondent les paroles
> Quand son nom gigantesque, entouré d'auréoles
> Se dresse dans mon vers de toute sa hauteur.'

At the end of 1828, the poet Barthélémy, who had already
published *Napoleon in Egypt*, went to Vienna and by the use of
considerable tact gained an entry into the study of Dietrichstein,
the Duke of Reichstadt's tutor, with a view to being received by
the Emperor's son.* The Austrian amiably agreed to discuss

---

* Auguste Barthélémy (1796–1867). An opponent of the Restoration, besides
Napoleon in Egypt and *Waterloo*, he wrote some violent satires aimed at the
King's ministers. Founder of the paper *Nemesis*, he also attacked Lamartine who
defended himself in the famous poem *Réponse à Némesis*.

poetry, but refused his request, saying that members of the Imperial Family were not in the habit of granting audiences.

'From that it would appear, Monsieur le Comte,' Barthélémy murmured, 'that Napoleon's son is not nearly as free as we in France imagine him to be.'

'The prince is not a prisoner,' hemmed Dietrichstein, 'but ... his situation is an unusual one.'

The poet left Vienna disappointed but inspired, and several months later published his *Le fils de l'homme, ou souvenirs ed Vienne*, whose success was so great that it resulted in his being dragged before a tribunal and condemned to three months imprisonment and 1,000 francs fine, for 'reviving and sustaining guilty recollections and hopes' – but his advocate did not miss the opportunity of getting in an effective retort to the magistrates:

'So one must not print the fact that HE has a son!'

Waste of effort, once more, in so far as Bonapartist propaganda was concerned, because this long poem, representing the hero's son as an Austrian archduke entirely ignorant of his father's history and indifferent to French affairs, was hardly designed to revive hopes.

However, the time was approaching when the old monarchy was to leave the stage, booed and jeered at by liberals, republicans and Bonapartists alike. 'There is still considerable disgust with the Bourbons and the King,' wrote Stendhal. 'It's the itch, everyone wants to be cured of it. My comparison is squalid, but it shows you the mixture of impatience and distaste that all this arouses.' History was advancing in seven-league boots: men like Clausel were now besieging the Chamber – Clausel who covered himself in glory in 1815 and was mentioned by the Emperor in his will – while Thiers' *Le National* openly sang the praises of the Conqueror, whose great shadow stood motionless and threatening, dominating the course of events. It only needed a shot to be fired.

III

1830

❋

'Débris du Grand Empire et de la Grande Armée
Colonne, d'où si haut parle la renommée.'

V. HUGO

On July 28, 1830, the tricolour flag floated over Notre-Dame and
the bell tolled the passing of a 1,000-year-old régime, whilst cries
of 'Hurrah for liberty!' and 'Down with the Charter!' drowned
those of 'Long live Napoleon II!' and 'Long live the Duc
d'Orléans!', or even lines from Béranger's *Old Flag*:

'Quand secouerai-je la poussière
Qui ternit ses nobles couleurs.'

Yet by August 9 Louis Philippe was King of the French. No
more Kings of France, no more divine right, but a liberal
monarchy in the English style, and it was not for this, surely, that
old soldiers, refugees and those persecuted under the Restoration
had fired their shot . . .

'Why should we fight?' asked an elderly workman.

'To defeat the Bourbons, and get rid of them.'

'Look how often we've been promised an end to them, yet here
they still are.'

'But today it's serious: don't you hear the rifle-fire and the big
guns?'

'Oh, it's serious is it?' cried the worthy man beginning to show
interest. 'I fought at Waterloo. Their provost-marshal condemned me to the galleys for shouting "Long live the Emperor!"

I've been waiting a long time. Now at last we'll square accounts with them.'*

And the brave fellow went and got killed on the Place de l'Hôtel-de-Ville, while under the Comtesse de Boigne's windows five verses of a song about Napoleon II were being sung:

'Sans le faire oublier, le fils vaudra le père.'

On July 27 a certain Chopin had had the audacity to appear in the Place de l'Odéon dressed in a way calculated to arouse excitement. Dumas describes the scene: 'He was dressed in a buttoned-up overcoat and cocked hat and riding a white horse. The resemblance to Napoleon was so striking that the whole crowd began to shout with one voice "Long live the Emperor."' A good woman of sixty took it more seriously: she fell on her knees and made the sign of the cross, declaring: 'Now I won't have to die without having seen him again.' It might have been possible to canalise this enthusiasm, discipline the veterans and besiege the throne, except for lack of a leader, a name, a sword. Gourgaud collected some Bonapartists together at his house, but what could he do against La Fayette, who already saw himself president of the future Republic, and Laffitte, who had sided with the Duc d'Orléans?†

So it was Philippe-Egalité's son whom La Fayette embraced on July 31 on the balcony of the Hôtel-de-Ville in front of a backdrop of tricolour flags 'Gilles Caesar's' accolade‡ took the place of a coronation. For Bonapartism had already become what it was to be for history, the cult of a unique Napoleon, and Thiers, whose ambition readily adapted itself to a bourgeois monarch, said hastily, as if to interpret the course of events: 'Napoleon II had nothing behind him but a few memories scattered here and there through town and country . . . His father's great glory has given him a purely imaginary power.'

* Vaulabelle: *Histoire des deux Restaurations.*

† Jacques Laffitte (1767–1844) Banker, governor of the Bank of France in 1814. Trustee for Napoleon's funds during his exile, then liberal deputy in 1816. President of the Council and Minister of Finance in 1830.

‡ 'Gilles Caesar' was one of La Fayette's nicknames.

The heir to that tremendous name, the young man to whom so many were turning their thoughts, but who had been diverted from his destiny by a misconceived education, by intrigues and hatred, sighed: 'As I am now I'm not fitted to be king of the French; I should be no match for the world and its flattery.'

His grandfather, the Emperor Francis, Marie-Louise and the Vienna court were not at all hostile to the idea of putting Napoleon's son on the throne of the Tuileries as soon as the way was cleared by the fall of Louis Philippe, which they hoped would not be far off, and for some time the poor Duke of Reichstadt let himself be deluded into a naif enthusiasm by drawing-room gossip. 'The chief object of my life is to be worthy of my father's glory; I believe I could attain this high purpose if some day I can succeed in developing only a few of his great qualities.' Metternich lost no time in throwing cold water on this smouldering fire, and using as intermediary an Austrian returned from Paris where he had been talking to Montholon, he painted a discouraging picture of Bonapartist feelings for the Duke's benefit.* Were there cries of 'Long live Napoleon II?' Perhaps, but the great Emperor's military glory was being used as a weapon against the last of the Bourbons. In fact the country was demanding liberty in equality, and the role of constitutional monarch could not fall to the conqueror's son. Besides, all true Bonapartists had already made their choice and announced their support for Louis Philippe.

The picture was only too lifelike, and the suspicious and orderly Orleanist bourgeoisie, backed by the bankers, had carried the day over the troops of the Empire, whose sole wealth lay in their fidelity. The strange régime was therefore supported on one side by great names that had helped win battles (Macdonald, Mortier, Oudinot and Molitor all signed the Proclamation of the

---

* This emissary, Prince Franz Josef Dietrichstein, had had searching discussions with Montholon and reported them to Metternich, with surprising cynicism. See Jean de Bourgoing's *Le Fils de Napoléon* (Payot.)

King) and on the other by financiers. (Laffitte was the first President of the Council under the July Monarchy, and the commission of July 29 counted three bankers among its seven members: Laffitte, Odier and Casimir Périer.)

To establish and maintain himself in power the new king, known in London as the 'cardboard king', had to become 'national', in other words liberal, and give pledges to the powerful opposition represented by Napoleon's army and administration. Officers who had been dismissed or put on half-pay would thus be reinstated: for instance Bertrand was made head of the Ecole Polytechnique, France's famous military academy, and then deputy for Indre, and Gourgaud became lieutenant-general and aide-de-camp to the King. Others, among them Stendhal, were given posts in the diplomatic service or prefectures. As Chateaubriand said mockingly: 'There are some men who have sworn fidelity in turn to the one and indivisible Republic, to the five persons of the Directory, to the three of the Consulate, to the one of the Empire, to the Additional Act at the time of the first Restoration, and now at the second Restoration have still something left for Louis Philippe. I am not as rich as that.' The Vicomte, a proud legitimist, surrendered all his functions and remained 'as naked as St. John'.

All this could not fail to encourage popular enthusiasm and give credit to the songs sung in the streets:

> 'Rendez-lui son petit chapeau
> Sa redingote grise
> Et sa noble devise.'

As early as 1831 Michelet noted the progress of the legend with a certain amount of irritation. After taking a stroll with a carpenter from the Ardennes he commented: 'On Sundays he reads the Bible, Vidocq, Simon de Nantua, Plutarch – but especially Bonaparte. The people's poetry is all to be found in Bonaparte.'

*　　　*　　　*

In the camp of the Napoleonides emotion was running high. In the absence of Napoleon II, the sons of Louis and Hortense were responsible for a spectacular project for a return to France.

'France has been delivered, our exile is over. The way to our native land lies open. It is for us to make every use of our opportunity.'

The chief of this scattered and sometimes irresponsible family, Madame Mère, did not share these youthful aspirations: she had seen too much and remembered too much to delude herself with hopes that anything could be expected from a popular movement more anti-Bourbon in character than Bonapartist. 'In proclaiming the Duc d'Orléans king before previously getting the nation's assent, the Chamber of deputies has broken all the principles of the Revolution and taken a terrible responsibility upon itself,' she wrote to Louis Napoleon. 'You write like a young hothead. To judge the situation correctly one must look at it coolly, and although I do not underestimate the vigour and courage of the people of Paris. I am far from seeing a philosophers' revolution in these battles bravely fought by a few Frenchmen ... Wait for events before judging them. You see I am preaching. I hope you won't take offence: it is only that an old head, cooled by experience and time, is trying to persuade a young and ardent head that is dear to her to see reason.'*

Laffitte, the President of the Council, although refusing to repeal the law of January 1816 exiling all the Bonapartes, announced himself ready to honour the treaty of Fontainebleau to ease difficult situations: it would only be necessary to formulate requests.† Madame Mère draped herself in antique dignity. 'It would be an outrage to the memory of the Emperor, and we would prove ourselves his son's worst enemies by such behaviour.

* Rome, August 17, 1830.

† The treaty of Fontainebleau, on April 11, 1814, after the first abdication, granted to Napoleon the sovereignty of the Isle of Elba, to Marie-Louise the Duchies of Parma and Piacenza, and to the members of the Imperial Family a sum of two and a half million francs in revenues or estates.

Besides, it would be remarkably despicable to beg from the government which upheld article 4 of the law of January 12, 1816, banishing us for ever.'* Hortense, who was ready to yield so as to improve a disastrous financial situation, was thoroughly scolded by her mother-in-law: 'Honour should always come before money. We must manage on what we have, and if we cannot live in royal style, let us live like honourable private individuals, rather than expose ourselves to humiliation and the reproaches of our conscience.'†

Like the most famous of her sons, this woman was carved all from one piece, and would never give way to advances; she proved this again when in 1834 the question arose of making an exception in her favour to the law of exile. 'Let them leave me with my honourable sufferings,' she wrote to a deputy, 'and carry my integrity of character to the grave, I will never let my own lot be separated from that of my children; it is the only consolation that remains to me.'‡

The others didn't always see things in the same light.§ Jérôme had been created Prince of Montfort by his father-in-law the King of Würtemberg who had treated him cavalierly in 1815; he was more interested in finance than in politics. Having toyed for a moment with the chimerical project of going to reign in Greece, he had settled in Rome, thanks to the support of his wife's cousin the Tsar and the generosity of his mother, who had paid for the move. Loans from his mother and the banks enabled him to maintain the court ceremonial he was so fond of: he ogled pretty girls, frequented the French Academy, which was dominated by Horace Vernet, visited his mother every day and sometimes Cardinal Fesch, his brother Lucien or Queen Hortense, but was careful not to give the slightest grounds for suspicion to the authorities of the Holy Alliance or the Vatican police, despite

* Letter to Julie Bonaparte, Comtesse de Survilliers, September 7, 1830.
† Letter to Hortense, Comtesse de Saint-Leu, September 15, 1830.
‡ Letter to the deputy Sapey, April 1834.
§ The family ranks had thinned: Elisa died in 1820, Napoleon in 1821, Eugène de Beauharnais in 1824 and Pauline in 1825.

leading the life of an exiled sovereign. His eldest son did not follow his example. Along with Hortense's sons, he had taken part in the demonstrations of December 1830, brandishing a tricolour flag in the streets of Rome and only escaping prison through the intervention of the Ministers of Russia and Würtemberg.

Lucien, former republican, devoted himself to expensive scientific distractions: astronomy in his observatory on the Adriatic or archaeology on his estate at Canino, and indulged all his weaknesses as foolishly as Jérôme, the most ruinous being his habit of buying land, villas and pictures with a view to selling them again when money was short. 'Since my revenue from Canino was reduced by half it isn't enough to pay the interest I owe my creditors,' he wrote to his brother Joseph in 1826, 'so I've been faced with the cruel necessity of declaring myself a bankrupt before the courts and asking for maintenance. This extremity, close as it is to insolvency, filled me with despair. Whether or no I still have bread to eat, God and perhaps my pen will nourish me.'

No one had much to say about Louis, who divided his time between Rome and Florence, while his two sons, Napoleon Louis and Louis Napoleon, belonged to the Carbonari, and gave the Vatican police a lot of trouble by intriguing to put Napoleon II on the throne of an independent Italy. The affair was rapidly beginning to become serious, and Austria was preparing to take repressive measures, but the elder died of some strange form of measles in 1831, and the younger, the future Napoleon III, fled from justice disguised as his mother's coachman and equipped with false papers. He had to wait twenty-one years to realise his ambition to occupy a throne – but then it was the throne of the Tuileries . . .

Joseph, who had gone to the United States in 1815, ruled in an easy-going way over an estate of some thousand hectares near Philadelphia, and all French refugees came to ring the bell at his gate. They were amiably received, and the ex-King of Spain did the honours of his house (the finest after the President's in the whole of the United States), showed them his Titians, Rubens and Velasquez, but his face clouded over and he became evasive as soon as someone proposed any enterprise that flavoured of political intrigue. The Emperor's death had made him head of the Bonaparte family, and it shocked him to hear that Louis Philippe had filched a crown to which he could himself lay claim, based on the instructions in his brother's will, as communicated to him by General Bertrand from London in October 1821: 'The Emperor said that the most important thing for his son was that he should never become a priest; that he should always be proud of being born a Frenchman ... that he should never do anything that might alienate or antagonise the French people.' These phrases, the banal interpretation of the dying man's intensely felt wishes, clearly affirmed the King of Rome's right to the succession, adding that King Joseph should be his mentor and support, until he came of age.

Joseph first laid his claim before the deputies of the new Chamber: 'An outlaw living far from my native soil, I would have come forward as soon as I got this letter, if I had not read, among so many names acknowledged by the liberality of the nation, that of a prince of the house of Bourbon ... It is impossible for princes born with a claim to rule their people, to rise above the prejudices of their birth. The Duc d'Orléans renounced his family at the time of their misfortunes. Is he less of a Bourbon thereby? No, Sirs, legitimacy belongs only to governments acknowledged by their nations. Nations create and destroy them according to their needs ... Napoleon's family has been summoned to power by 3,500,000 votes. Napoleon II was proclaimed in 1815. I have certain information to show that Napoleon II will be worthy of France ... Until Austria gives him back to France, I offer myself to share your dangers, your efforts, your work, and, on his arrival, to hand over to him the wishes, the example and the last will and testament of his father.' This message was backed by a direct appeal to La Fayette, Thibaudeau, to Generals Lamarque, Gérard, Jourdan, Belliard, Merlin, the Duke of Padua and Count

Roederer, and by a discreet approach by General Lallemand to Vienna and Parma.*

Madame Mère, who refused to ask favours, and the philosopher King, who preferred talking of dynastic successions rather than pensions and rents, took the same line without previous discussion: they were the only members of the family whose idea of the imperial heritage had a certain dignity.

*   *   *

Metternich had said of the Duke of Reichstadt: 'He must be excluded from all thrones, once and for all,' so it was with a sour expression that he heard early in 1832 that the instability of the

* Thibaudeau, Count of the Empire, a member of the Chamber of Peers in 1815, where he was noticed for his opposition to the Bourbons.

General Lamarque had been noticed by Napoleon at Austerlitz; he was governor of Paris, and general-in-chief of the army of the Vendée. Outlawed in 1815, and one of the opposition deputies on his return to France, he took an active part in the 1830 Revolution, opposing Louis Philippe. His funeral in June 1832 was the signal for a popular rising.

General Gérard, Count of the Empire, deprived of his posts by Louis XVIII. Opposition deputy in 1822, he was Minister for War and Grand Chancellor of the Legion of Honour under Louis Philippe, and senator under Napoleon III.

Marshal Jourdan had been military councillor to King Joseph in Spain. Going over to the Bourbons, he had however refused to preside over the council of war called to judge Marshal Ney. Louis Philippe made him Governor of the Invalides.

General Belliard had been governor of Madrid during Joseph's rule in Spain. Exiled in 1815, he was an enthusiastic supporter of the July Revolution.

Count Merlin had served in the kingdom of Naples and afterwards in Spain. Louis Philippe nominated him to a military post in Corsica.

Arrighi, Duke of Padua, ally of the Bonapartes, had been secretary to Joseph's embassy at Rome, and also served in Spain. In 1849 he was deputy for Corsica in the legislative assembly, and later senator under Napoleon III.

Count Roederer, attached to Bonaparte since the 18 Brumaire; he was Minister of Finance at Naples under King Joseph, and then Secretary of State of the Grand Duchy de Berg. Member of the Chamber of Peers during the Hundred Days, he returned there under the July monarchy.

General Lallemand a friend of King Joseph's since the Spanish war. He rallied to Napoleon during the Hundred Days and was created Peer of France. Condemned to death during the Restoration, he took refuge in the United States. Louis Philippe gave him back his rank and his place in the Chamber of Peers.

political situation in Paris gave cause to fear a Bonapartist *coup* inspired by Generals Lamarque and Clauzel, backed by the garrisons of east France, and by old La Fayette, an opponent of Louis Philippe's, but he was too cautious and crafty to reveal his batteries openly, and too inquisitive not to listen to messengers from the conspirators. First came Montholon to tell him that those loyal to the Emperor were committing themselves to proclaiming Napoleon II as soon as the young prince appeared at Strasburg, but Metternich was on the war-path: 'After six months the Duke of Reichstadt will be surrounded by ambitious demands, hatred and compromises ... Bonapartism without Bonaparte is an absolutely false concept. Napoleon succeeded in dominating and subduing the French Revolution with a genius we are not likely to come across again, but even he profited from a combination of circumstances favouring his plans. In the present state of affairs, what could Bonaparte himself do surrounded by a mob whose suspicions and puerile vanity would kill a reputation in twenty-four hours? Napoleon rebuilt an edifice from the materials of a destroyed social order, but you are determined to destroy even the debris. Greatness seldom passes from father to son.'

A little later, it was the turn of Fouché's son, Athanase d'Otrante, now a Swedish subject, to present himself at the chancellery, straight from the United States where he had been consulting with King Joseph: he made suggestions about establishing the ex-King in the realm of the Emperor of Austria, and spoke at greater length about the future of the Duke of Reichstadt. At the same time Marie-Louise, who believed she had thrown a veil of oblivion over the past, choked with rage when she got a message from her brother-in-law concerning the best means of re-establishing her son on the throne of the Tuileries.

'These people can never keep quiet,' she complained.

It was too much, and when in his turn Lucien requested a passport in order to come and discuss with the Austrian chancellor the rights and chances of his brother's son, he was told bluntly that by decision of the Holy Alliance members of the family were forbidden to travel without the authorisation of the great powers.

* * *

On January 25, 1831, His Britannic Majesty's ambassador at Vienna gave a ball which excited much interest. Couples were dancing, ladies chattering, and diplomats formed groups apart, when all heads turned towards the door to see the long expected and first official appearance of the Duke of Reichstadt. He was nearly twenty years old, tall, slender and handsome; he was said to be reserved, sometimes melancholy, but he was Napoleon's son and that was enough to move some, intrigue others, and give the ambassadors a chance to send home spicy dispatches. Among the crowd, one man in a great state of emotion followed with his eyes that tall slender figure, with narrow shoulders and a rather feminine profile – it was Marshal Marmont, Duke of Ragusa, who had been driven from Paris by the July Revolution, and become intimate with Metternich and a familiar figure at the Vienna Court. The Duke of Reichstadt, dressed in the uniform of a lieutenant-colonel of the Nassau infantry, held himself more stiffly than usual, to overcome his timidity. 'He seemed to me to have his father's gaze,' noted Marmont, 'and that was his chief resemblance. His eyes are smaller than Napoleon's and more deepset, but they have the same expression, the same fire, the same energy. There was resemblance too in the lower part of the face and chin. Finally his complexion was like Napoleon's when a young man. The same pallor and the same colour of skin; but all the rest of his figure was like his mother and the house of Austria. He was taller than Napoleon by about five inches.'

The Count of Dietrichstein, his tutor, circled round his pupil, pink with delight and repeating words of advice:

'You aren't talking enough ... you aren't holding yourself properly ... you are too familiar.'

Among the guests were two princes of the House of Bourbon, Louis Philippe's ambassador and the representative of Charles X, and it was important for the pupil to make a good impression. Suddenly the prince stopped in front of the man who had been pointed out as Marshal Marmont and said amiably:

'I am charmed to see one of my father's earliest companions in arms.'*

The French newspapers described the evening thus: 'The Duke has just made his entry into the social world; he has an extremely pleasant appearance, and those who talked to him found that he had a lot of common sense. He studies military matters with great assiduity and has a remarkable knowledge of everything that concerns his father's history.'

Three days later, hoping that this diversion would drive the rumours from Paris into the background, Metternich sent the Duke of Ragusa to the Hofburg to tell the young man Napoleon's story.

'Don't forget to describe the wars as they really were and make his son realise how excessive was his ambition and how dire the results,' the chancellor advised.

The young Duke was not taken in: 'Marmont wants to kill three birds with one stone,' he confided to his friend Prokesch: 'to let Metternich understand that he will serve his political aims, to induce Louis Philippe to get in touch with him as soon as possible, and in case of my fate taking me back to France, to pose as my friend and secret protector. I need his help to make myself known to the French. All the same, if I ascend the throne I shall throw him out.'

Metternich showed little understanding of the character of this youth, who was already in a fever as a result of the situation. The

---

* It is known that after the surrender of Essonnes, which delivered Paris to the Allies in 1814, Napoleon had accused Marmont of treason. Louis XVIII created him peer of France and Chevalier de Saint-Louis. Governor of Paris in 1831, he was brutally rigorous in defence of Charles X's cause, and fled the capital never to return.

Marshal's story, resounding with the rumble of cannonfire, horses galloping, the clank of arms and his father's dry voice, was designed to exalt his mood and goad him to action. He remembered what his grandfather, Francis, had said:

'If the people of France ask for you, and if the Allies give their consent, I would not be against your occupying the French throne.'

There were too many 'ifs' in this supposition. And the chancellor understood matters differently.

When unrest broke out in Italy in 1831, the revolutionaries of Modena, tired of the despotism of the Hapsburg Francis IV, proclaimed Napoleon II King of Italy and Metternich had to face the situation.

'It's a revolution of Bonapartists supported by French anarchists,' he declared, hoping to spread fear among all the Courts of Europe.

These anarchists were more dangerous than the young prince who coughed at the first touch of cold weather; they were looking too often towards Paris in fact, and the Austrian chancellor decided to carry out a dramatic diplomatic *coup*. The son of Eugène de Beauharnais had designs on the throne of Belgium, in spite of the fact that Louis Philippe coveted that kingdom for one of his own sons: Vienna therefore insinuated that, as King of Italy, Napoleon II would be just as troublesome to France as it would be for Austria to have the Duke of Leuchtenberg at Brussels. The Austrian ambassador at Paris exaggerated this threat by showing Louis Philippe King Joseph's letters to Metternich, and the reports made by the Austrian minister at Florence of the guilty activities of Queen Hortense's sons in Italy. It was enough to cure the 'cardboard king' of opposing Austrian activities against the Carbonari and the old soldiers or functionaries of the Napoleonic era, the true instigators of trouble in the peninsula.

The Duke knew nothing of these correspondences, and his only idea was to fly to Parma and defend the rights of the insignificant Marie-Louise: he was refused even this harmless honour, but to soothe the wound to his pride the Emperor Francis confided to him genially:

'If you even appeared on the pont de Strasburg in Paris it would be all up with the Orléans family.'

IV

A WAVE OF BONAPARTISM

*

'A thousand cannons lie sleeping in that name (Napoleon)
and in the column in the Place Vendôme, and if those thousand
cannons were to wake one day, the Tuileries would tremble.'
H. HEINE

After a law had been passed authorising those outlawed by the
Restoration to return to their towns and villages, in September
1830 the Chamber of Deputies accepted a petition, backed by
General Lamarque, to ask England to return Napoleon's ashes
from St. Helena. This was acting quickly, and Chateaubriand,
who was doubtful whether 'this homely, domestic monarchy
could please liberty-lovers for long', jeered cruelly at the project
in his pamphlet on the banishment of Charles X, reasoning with a
spirit by no means devoid of logic: 'Why forbid the relations of
the man who dominated Europe to enter France, and yet open the
door to his ashes? The latter are much more dangerous . . . They
will become active at every anniversary of their victories; every
day, from under their column they will say to every quasi-legiti-
mist passer-by: What have you done with our national honour?'

In vain Lamarque fashioned moving phrases to beg that 'under
the weeping escort of his old companions in arms, he who so
often returned to France in a triumphal chariot should now
return in his coffin'. The King had got the petition rejected by
deputies who were as afraid as he was of the triumphal entry into
Paris of these embarrassing remains, to the great indignation of
Victor Hugo:

'Oh! Quand tu bâtissais de ta main colossale
Pour ton trône appuyée sur l'Europe vassale
Ce pilier souverain,
Ce bronze devant qui tout n'est que poudre et sable
Sublime monument deux fois impérissable,
Fait de gloire et d'airain,
Oh! qui t'eût dit alors, à ce faîte sublime,
Tandis que tu rêvais sous ce trophée opime
Un avenir si beau,
Qu'un jour à cet affront il te faudrait descendre,
Que trois cents avocats oseraient à ta cendre
Chicaner ce tombeau.'

There was similar opposition in September 1831, when the question was again submitted to the Chamber.

'Napoleon curbed anarchy,' cried La Fayette; 'his ashes must not be allowed to come and increase it today!'

On the other hand the Bonapartists were gratified by the order of April 8, 1831, due to Casimir Périer, authorising the replacement of Napoleon's statue on the Vendôme column, and also by an issue by the Mint of 165 coins recalling the great dates of the Consulate and the Empire. But was so much bronze really needed to renew the conqueror's sway over the capital – this conqueror who came alive again every evening on the stage, reaping applause just as he used to at reviews at the Tuileries? Several weeks after the *Three Glorious Days*, the Cirque d'Hiver had advertised *Crossing the St. Bernard* and the whole season had been dedicated to the Emperor.

At the Vaudeville it was *Bonaparte, lieutenant of Artillery*, at the Ambigu-Comique: *Napoleon*, at the Variétés: *Napoleon at Berlin or the grey overcoat*, at the Porte Saint-Martin: *Napoleon or Schoenbrunn and St. Helena*. In this last piece the rôle of the hero was played by a certain Gobert: his talent was small but his resemblance such that the old soldiers who acted as supers needed no persuasion, and Mademoiselle George wept in her box. At the end of another performance the actor who took the part of Hudson

Lowe only got home with police protection. Soon the Nouveautés announced *Bonaparte at school at Brienne*; *Josephine or the return from Wagram* at the Opéra-Comique with music by Adam; *Malmaison and St. Helena* at the Gaîté; and elsewhere *The grenadier of Wagram*, *The grenadier of the Isle of Elba*, and finally in January 1831, as the pièce de resistance, Alexandre Dumas' *Napoleon Bonaparte*, with a preface in which the author apologised for letting himself catch the infection: 'I am the son of the republican general Alexandre Dumas, who died in 1806 in disgrace with the Emperor.' The play had six acts and twenty-four tableaux, eighty or ninety speaking characters, and the production cost 100,000 francs; it was written in eight days. 'It's not good,' the author admitted, 'it can't be helped but the title is sure to give it a topical success.' Lemaître brought the Emperor to life again, and wrote an interminable melodrama six times as long as one of Racine's tragedies – an event in Parisian life but a flop all the same; and Stendhal, who was dying of cold and boredom in his Trieste consulate, said triumphantly 'I *foretold* in 1826 that such a play would be written and that before ten years were up the political circumstances would make it possible to stage it. And then people say I've got no sense.'

There was even a vaudeville at the Gaîté called *Napoleon in paradise*, whose last lines, recited by a soldier of the Old Guard to an astonished St. Peter, made the audience shout with joy:

> 'Vous craignez qu'un jour de goguette
> Le Caporal dise au Bon Dieu:
> Ote-toi de là que je m'y mette.'

*   *   *

Queen Hortense was on her way back from Italy with her younger son, pursued by the Austrian police after the insurrection in the Romagna, and dropped out of the clouds into Paris in 1831, entering by the same rue Mouffetard through which she had escaped sixteen years earlier under the protection of some allied officers. She returned with a beating heart, full of nostalgic memories, having followed a veritable pilgrimage from the frontier by way of Fréjus, Aix, Avignon, Montélimar and Lyons. She stopped to visit the Palace at Fontainebleau, wearing a veil so as not to be recognised by the servants who had waited on her in the old days, and lingered in the Court of Farewells, in the chapel where her son (who was delighted to be exploring France at her side) had been baptised in 1810 along with twenty-two children of princes and marshals to whom the Emperor and Marie-Louise stood godparents, and finally in her own room, which had been the Duc de Berri's since 1810. In Paris she went to the Hôtel de Hollande, rue de la Paix, whence she saw the Place Vendôme and the column. One evening Louis Philippe received her discreetly at the Palais Royal, saying as she came in that he 'knew from experience all the sadness of exile'. He seemed anxious to sweeten her lot, and accepted her alibi of wanting to take the cure at Vichy.

'It will be thought perfectly natural, and then you can prolong your stay, or else come back; in this country people get used to things very quickly, everything is forgotten at once.'

The President of the Council, Casimir Périer, visited her in her rooms to discuss some financial claims that were troubling her, and gave her a viaticum of 16,000 francs on the King's behalf.

On May 4, the eve of the anniversary of Napoleon's death, she hurried to the *Diorama*, where a picture by Daguerre was shown, representing the tomb on St. Helena; she mingled with the deeply moved crowd, to meditate before this striking representation of the deserted valley where England believed that the man and his ideas had been buried together.* Like everyone else, she heard that a group of Bonapartists had ordered from Saint Mandé a statue of wood destined to be placed on the Vendôme Column until the final definitive figure was ready, and that the police were

---

* Dioramas, with their historical tableaux, were all the rage at the time: *The Tomb on St. Helena* had been honoured by a visit from the King and Queen Amélie that April.

instructed to stop it entering the barriers of the Capital. While she wrote to Madame Mère to tell her this news, Prince Louis who was ill, got someone to read him the *Ode to the Column*:

> 'Dors! nous t'irons chercher! Ce jour viendra peut-être!
> Car nous t'avons pour dieu sans t'avoir eu pour maître;
> Oh! vas, nous te ferons de belle funérailles!
> Et nous t'amènerons la jeune poésie
>   Chantant la jeune liberté.'

The crowd in the streets grew bigger, and moved towards the Place Vendôme, tolerantly watched by the royal troops. In a few moments the four eagles on the monument had disappeared beneath flowers and garlands. People sang the *Marseillaise*, and cried 'Long live the Emperor!', and the National Guard led by the brave Mouton had to bring their water-pumps into action. The future emperor lay in his room suffering from measles, and started up at every shout, taking it as an encouragement from fate.

'If I hadn't been ill on May 5th,' he said later, 'and if I had gone to the Place Vendôme and shouted "Long live Napoleon II", everyone would have followed me. Louis Philippe knew this and that's why he saw to it that I left.'

A rumour going the rounds that the Prince had been recognised on the Place Vendôme, caused Casimir Périer to visit the ex-Queen of Holland in person and beg her to start on her return journey.†

A few days later the two fugitives arrived in London, a city full of memories of Napoleon, and where the arbiter of good taste was

---

* Mouton, Comte de Lobeau (1770–1838) had been aide-de-camp to Bonaparte, and distinguished himself at Austerlitz, Jena, in Poland and Spain. Taken prisoner at Waterloo, he did not escape being outlawed by Louis XVIII, but Louis Philippe restored his rank and appointed him commander of the National Guard, before making him marshal in 1831. Napoleon said of him: 'He's a lion in a sheep's skin.'

† Louis Philippe made everything easy for the journey, providing passports when she wanted to leave England, where she had gone on her way to Switzerland.

Prince de Talleyrand, former minister of the Empire and now
ambassador to the King of the French ... Nine years earlier
Chateaubriand had also shown surprise at the sight of this austere
capital besotted with Bonaparte. 'They moved from denigration
of *Nic* to a foolish enthusiasm,' he noted. 'Memoirs of Bonaparte
proliferated; his bust was on every chimney-piece; engravings of
him illuminated the windows of every print shop; his colossal
statue by Canova adorned the Duke of Wellington's staircase.
Might not another sanctuary in the temple have been dedicated to
Mars in chains? This deification seems more appropriate to a vain
caretaker than to an honourable warrior. General, you didn't
conquer Napoleon at Waterloo. All you did was wrench asunder
the last link in an already broken chain of destiny.'

In 1828 the Marquis de Custine was also amazed to find that
the Emperor had become a 'hero of melodrama and pantomime',
and sat enthroned in all the smart shops, either cast in bronze or
engraved in copper.*

This devil of a man, described by the poet Landor† as 'a mortal
man beyond mortal praise', conquered London before Paris, and
in his refutation of Walter Scott's biography, Hazlitt‡ was not
afraid to say that the sun of Austerlitz had not yet set. It was still
shining in his own heart, and for him the Son of Glory was not
dead and never would be.

The ex-Queen of Holland was invited to every London reception to talk about court life at the Tuileries, and Napoleon, and
the brilliant days she would never forget. Lady Glengall met her,
and in her presence evoked with wonder the conqueror's image:

* The Marquis de Custine (1790–1857), whose father and grandfather had
perished on the revolutionary scaffold, was the son of Delphine de Sabran, friend
of Chateaubriand until 1805. Involved with all the Romantics from Lamartine to
Chopin, from Stendhal to Hugo, he left novels and poetry and also some interesting travel books: *Spain under Ferdinand VII* and *Russia in 1839.*

† Walter Savage Landor (1775–1864). A fierce opponent of Napoleon, he raised
at his own expense a corps of volunteers to defend Spain against the French armies
in 1808.

‡ William Hazlitt (1778–1830) critic and essayist, author of a *Life of Napoleon
Buonaparte.*

his fine profile, like a Roman Emperor's, would lend itself well to sculpture; she remembered his beautiful teeth and his gay, sweet smile – like that of a child rather than the master of the world.

All the Napoleons who had figured on the Parisian stage went their rounds likewise on the banks of the Thames: the Surrey theatre put on *Bonaparte, lieutenant of Artillery*, while *Crossing the St. Bernard* was shown at the Vaudeville and Astley's. Prince Louis, although barely recovered from jaundice, hurried to Covent Garden to see a series of tableaux representing the Emperor's life, and was amazed to find that St. Helena had been prudishly suppressed, and that the performance ended with his farewells at Fontainebleau . . .

*   *   *

In Vienna, Metternich was furious at having to put up with this wave of Bonapartism on the rebound, for he was bombarded by accurate reports of surprising proposition made by Montholon to Bombelles, Austrian minister at Berne.* The Emperor's companion in exile, temporarily settled in Switzerland, declared that he was acting as intermediary for the deputy François Mauguin, and spoke out confidently: in return for Austrian help in installing Napoleon II on the French throne, the truth about current Italian, German and Belgian troubles – the work of secret societies under the control of a mysterious personage† – would be revealed.

Metternich was later informed that King Jérôme had approached the Austrian minister at Florence with a view to sending an emissary to the Emperor Francis to discuss the future of the Duke of Reichstadt. Another individual, describing himself as having been sent by King Joseph, desired an audience with the Duke himself. He guaranteed that Louis Philippe would be

* He was the brother of Charles de Bombelles, Grand Master of Ceremonies of the Austrian court, whom Marie-Louise married secretly in 1834, after Neipperg's death.

† This was that same Mauguin, whom Guizot described as 'a sophist-advocate, supporting an ambitious and warlike policy'.

overthrown before March 1932, that the Duc de Bordeaux would not be acceptable to the nation, and that a republic would constitute a threat to all the monarchies on the continent.*

One day Metternich read that Montholon had in fact brought a letter from Prince Louis addressed to Napoleon's son: 'My dear cousin, having for the first time found a safe means of getting a letter to you, I eagerly seize this opportunity to express to you the tender feelings of attachment I have preserved towards you ever since my childhood. What pleasure it has given me to hear you praised, and how happy I should be to be able to give you proofs of my devotion! I hope that a day will come when a less cruel fate allows me once again to see the son of the man who was the constant object of our reverence and all our love, so that I may express to you by word of mouth the sincere feelings I have for you.'

Nothing suspicious surely in this declaration of allegiance to the direct heir of the family name, designed also to obliterate recollections of the unfortunate incidents in Romagna, and certain other activities of a man who was acting as if he were the head of the dynasty, yet Metternich flew into a rage, and filed away both reports and letters, after communicating their drift to Louis Philippe, whom he had finally decided to accept as King of the French.

'Here,' he assured the ambassador of France benignly, 'we are all Philippe, from head to toe.'

The Duke of Reichstadt, who was kept in ignorance of all these comings and goings, interviews and dispatches, often talked about the future to his friend Prokesch, who seemed to have taken his tune from the Emperor Francis, and be scraping away at the same refrain.† 'My advice was, and still is, that once Louis Philippe

* The Duc de Bordeaux, future Comte de Chambord, grandson of Charles X. The candidate of the legitimists, he died in exile in 1883.

† Anton Prokesch von Osten (1795–1876) had been aide-de-camp to Schwartzenberg and had published an account of the Napoleonic campaigns. His role as intimate of the Duke of Reichstadt, who was warmly attached to this older man, remains mysterious – half-way between friendship and intrigue. After the Duke's

has been overthrown,' he wrote confidently, 'anarchy will follow, and only then will Napoleon's son become king or emperor, gratifying equally the desires of France and the other powers.' Unfortunately for the Duke, the government of the 'cardboard king' hung on, under the guidance of the inflexible Casimir Périer, defending itself against right and left with cunning and skill. When it got wind of intrigues leading to an attempted rising at Strasburg – a place where Napoleon's son could appear 'alone and unarmed' some fine day – and of secret correspondence between Queen Hortense and Prince Louis mentioning Napoleon II by name, it raised the question of the law of April 10, 1832, designed to prolong the exile of both Bonapartes and Bourbons, and prevent the former owning estates or revenues in France.

The time had come to sound people's attitudes, and sum them up ... When Thiers declared bluntly: 'Napoleon stood alone; after him, nothing – absolutely nothing,' voices were raised here and there, some among the legitimists, some among the Bona-partists. Martignac, a former minister of Charles X, condemned the principle of banishment itself: 'In 1815, after a price had been set on Napoleon's head, did it not reappear encircled by the imperial crown? And those Bourbons, banished in perpetuity at the same time, weren't they back a few days later in the palace of their ancestors?' Someone else said mockingly: 'You have claimed Napoleon's ashes, and you want to restore that colossus to the column in the Place Vendôme. Can you at the same time hand over his family to banishment?' The son of the minister of public worship under the Empire, Portalis, who had been disgraced by Napoleon before becoming Charles X's Foreign Secretary, raised his voice against this ostracism in the name of glory: 'When I speak of Napoleon, it is not his son I am thinking of. Like all great military leaders, Napoleon has no posterity but his victories.'

The Emperor's son was not to suffer long from such pettinesses,

---

death, this diplomat, who was not lacking in ambition, had a distinguished career, and represented Austria in Greece: Prussia and Turkey.

nor from the bans imposed on him by the country of his birth. Ever since July 1830, his doctor had passed through all the torments of ignorance when auscultating him, diagnosing first 'a lack of development in the pectoral organs' – while the young man, unusually disturbed by puberty, and obsessed by stories of his father's death, thought he had some disease of stomach or liver – and later believing in an affection of the skin, for which he prescribed salt baths, and milk and soda-water to drink. All this time the invalid coughed and was feverish, felt languid and yet furious not to be able to share the life of the Wasa regiment, of which his grandfather had just made him second-in-command. In January 1832 he complained of a chill contracted during a military ceremony, was treated for 'the bile' and suffered also from outgrowing his strength so that he looked thinner and more hollow-chested every day; he had to stay in his gloomy rooms at the Hofburg, and try to keep boredom at bay by watching the guard march past, or observing the arrival and departure of visitors and the glittering uniforms of dignitaries and officers: he had become simply a forehead 'glued to the window-pane'. His confidant, Prokesch, had just been given a mission to Italy, his aunt the Archduchess Sophie, who lent a possibly too tender ear to his troubles, was travelling in Hungary, and he was left with no companions except his tutor and his military household.

The last pleasure he enjoyed was given him by Louis Marchand, his father's valet, who had witnessed the agony of St. Helena and who wrote to him on March 18, 1832: 'For several years I have been requesting permission to hand over to your Imperial Highness certain objects of sentimental value, entrusted to me by your August Father, the Emperor Napoleon, during his last moments at St. Helena. Convinced as I am that Your Highness must wish to identify yourself in spirit with them, and having had no reply to my requests, I am addressing myself to you, Prince, in hopes that you will make known your orders to me, and that I may conform to the last wishes of the Emperor my master, and have the honour to be allowed to hand to you in person that which has been entrusted to me.' Alas, a note from Metternich prevented Marchand's move having any result . . .

Like a wounded animal, the invalid went to ground at Schoenbrunn. It was his last journey and, as if to make his end even more solitary, the chancellor kept back all the letters that poured in signed by Napoleon's last companions at St. Helena, and by Prince Louis, who spoke for all the Bonapartes: 'Ah, if the presence of a nephew of your father's could do you any good, if the attentions of a friend who bears your name could ease your sufferings a little . . . I hope my letter will fall into the hands of someone compassionate.' It was too late: on June 13 the Duke spat blood; on the 20th he received the sacrament in the company of the Archduchess Sophie – who was very soon to give birth to the Archduke Maximilian – and on June 24 Marie-Louise arrived from Parma to see him die. On July 22 his life ended in the room where his father had slept after Austerlitz and Wagram, breathing his last sad words in German. His remains were to rest in the gloomy, romantic crypt of the church of the Capuchins in Vienna (the mausoleum of the Imperial Austrian Family) enclosed in a bronze sarcophagus ornamented with lions' heads and symbols of war. The lid bore the Latin inscription: 'To the eternal memory of Joseph-Charles-Francis, Duke of Reichstadt, son of Napoleon, Emperor of the French, born in Paris on March 20, 1811, given the title of King of Rome in his cradle. Endowed with every quality of mind and body, remarkable for the elegance of his figure, the great beauty of his features, the unusual grace of his language, for his studies and his literary work, he was attacked by phthisis in the flower of his age, and a tragic death carried him away in the Emperor's castle of Schoenbrunn, near Vienna, on July 22, 1832.'

Metternich had not waited for this premature death to speculate as to its political results. 'The Duke of Reichstadt's illness is a typical case of pulmonary phthisis, and if this is a ruthless disease at any age, it is fatal at twenty-one.' he had written to his ambassador in Paris. 'I beg you to persuade King Louis Philippe to pay attention to the person who will succeed the Duke. I use the word *succession*, because in the Bonapartist hierarchy there is a succession openly avowed and respected by the party. Louis Bonaparte is a young man thoroughly involved in the intrigues of the sect; he is not safeguarded by the Emperor's principles like the Duke of Reichstadt. On the day the Duke dies, he will consider himself called to the head of the French Republic.'

Time was to prove him right.

*   *   *

Madame Mère had received Prokesch at the Rinuccini Palace on the evening before July 22: she pestered him with questions about the handsome blond boy, whom she always referred to as the Roi de Rome, and she wept to hear his intelligence and charm praised, and his attachment to memories of his childhood.

'He must respect his father's last wishes; his hour will come, and he will ascend the paternal throne.'

She stood up with difficulty, and placed her blind woman's hands on the forehead of the young man, who knelt before her.

'As I cannot go to him, may your head receive the blessing of his grandmother, who will soon leave this world. My prayers, my tears, my wishes will be with him until my last moment. Take him what I have placed on your head, what I entrust to your heart.'

A few days later a letter from Marie-Louise came to plunge the tragic palace in mourning once again.

'In the hope of softening the bitterness of the sad news that it is my unfortunate duty to announce to you, I would not yield to anyone else the painful task of communicating it. On Sunday 22, at five o'clock in the morning, my beloved son the Duke of Reichstadt succumbed to his long and cruel sufferings. I had the consolation of being with him during his last moments, and also of being able to convince myself that nothing had been neglected that could have saved his life. But medical aid was impotent against a disease of the chest which from the first the doctors unanimously judged so dangerous that it must infallibly carry my son to the grave at an age when he aroused the fairest hopes. It was God's will. For us nothing remains but to submit, and to mingle our sorrow and our tears.'

Madame Mère accepted this fresh bereavement with Christian submission, but since her daughter-in-law's behaviour inspired her with neither the gentleness nor affection necessary, Cardinal Fesch replied in her name:

'In spite of the political blindness which has always interfered with my receiving news of the beloved child whose loss you have announced, I have never ceased having a mother's entrails towards him. He was still an object of some consolation to me, but at my great age, it has been God's will to add this blow to my other painful infirmities. I beg you to accept my gratitude, Madame, for taking the trouble in such painful circumstances to ease the bitterness of my soul. Rest assured that it will persist throughout my life. Since my state of health makes it impossible for me to sign this letter, permit me to entrust my brother with the task.'

The French newspapers silenced their tirades to deplore the death of this French archduke, cradled in glory, but with solitude as his inheritance. The *Revue des Deux Mondes* wrote: 'He is dead, the poor young man, because he devoured his own substance, because he lacked fresh air in that royal court which became his prison. He is dead because, seeing himself forgotten by France in 1830, he had no hope for the future.' The *Constitutionnel* moralised: 'This obscure end to a life showing promise of such fine qualities, this last pale ray from an immense glory that has just been extinguished, is a sad subject for meditation.' But it did not forget to add that 'Napoleon II had numerous supporters in some parts of France at least. Factions will go on disputing his heritage among themselves and with the government, and it will fall to the man who can rally the mass of the people in the true interests of the country.' *Le Moniteur*, reflecting official opinion, was content with a few unctuous phrases: 'The mere fact that a young man's life has been snuffed out a little after his twentieth year, and that a famous name for which so great a future had once been foretold has so quickly ended, so quickly became a part of history, arouses a sad emotion which is sure to be unanimously shared.' Louis Philippe proclaimed his sincere grief, and saw that a letter of condolence was sent to the Emperor of Austria by Queen Amélie, according to court protocol.

In the ranks of the old imperial army and throughout the French countryside the news aroused a more genuine emotion, as was witnessed by Heinrich Heine on a journey through Normandy: 'In every cottage there is a picture of the Emperor's son, crowned with everlasting flowers like the Saviour's in Holy Week. Many soldiers wore black crêpe bands. An old man with a wooden leg shook my hand sadly, saying: "Now it's all over."' Victor Hugo immortalised in his inimitable style the end of this line:

'Tous deux sont morts – Seigneur votre droite est terrible.
Vous avez commencé par le maître invincible
    Par l'homme triomphant;
Puis vous avez enfin complété l'ossuaire
Dix ans vous ont suffi pour filer le suaire
    Du père et de l'enfant.'

This sudden death, rousing suspicions of poison in some, occurred just when Bonapartist sentiments were being most loudly expressed, and when Napoleon's son could have been induced to play a part in French affairs. On May 4, 1832, the Paris police had arrested some people who were about to decorate the column with flowers, to mark the eleventh anniversary of the Emperor's death. A month later the funeral procession of General Lamarque – a victim of cholera like Casimir Périer – plunged the capital in fire and blood. Lamarque, who had defeated Sir Hudson Lowe at the siege of Capri, the splendid fighter of Wagram, died regretting his inability to avenge his country 'for the infamous treaties of 1814 and 1815', and was thought of by the people as the

survivor of those epic days, the man who had the courage to
declare in 1830, during the debate about the Return of the Ashes:
'Everything to do with Napoleon is great; there is power in his
name, his memory is a cult, death has not been able to freeze his
ashes.' In the retinue which followed his coffin on June 5, Bonapartists, republicans and extremists walked side by side, and
noisily insisted on making a detour to the column. One or two
wild spirits brandished a red flag, and in no time Paris was
plunged in bloody confusion lasting two long days. Repression
was brutal, martial law was declared, and the police complacently
settled their account with the republican faction, who, for lack of
an effective leader, expressed their opposition by yelling the name
'Napoleon!' 'A thousand cannons lie sleeping in that name,'
wrote Heinrich Heine, 'and in the column in the Place Vendôme,
and if those thousand cannons were to wake one day the Tuileries
would tremble.'

Who could unloose such a storm of bronze? With Napoleon's
son dead, under the terms of the Senatus consult of May 18, 1804,
the succession passed to Joseph and then Louis, and to their male
heirs.*

On July 20, two days before the Duke of Reichstadt's death,
the ex-King of Spain had embarked at Philadelphia for Europe,
and on August 15 he arrived at Liverpool and was informed of
the death of this nephew, whose rights he had come to support
and whose plans he intended to encourage at the request of many
partisans. His meeting with Prince Louis, who was posing as
claimant, naturally lacked warmth . . . The young man certainly
seemed on first acquaintance 'gentle, amenable, industrious,
honourable and full of delicacy', but he very soon revealed that
he also had a dangerous mania for launching on shadowy projects,
and Joseph saw him leave for Switzerland with a good deal of
relief.

---

* Joseph only had daughters: Zénaide, married to Lucien's son, and Charlotte,
widow of Napoleon-Louis, eldest son of the ex-King of Holland and Queen
Hortense.

As he was forbidden to go to Italy by the Viennese court, the philosopher-king made London his home and lived there for three years, devoting his energy and money to defending his brother's memory by his pen: 'He was neither a parricide, nor a despot, nor yet a tyrant. He was what his times and the nation wanted. He would have been the Titus or Trajan of that century in Rome, Washington in America, Charlemagne in the eighth century. In all he did of good or ill in his time, he had one great accomplice: the French people.' This was his theme, and it did not lack skill. It is by associating the French nation to the great deeds of the Empire as well as to its errors, that one can in fact impose the image of a sovereign confirmed by the people's will in a triumphant plebiscite; it was a thesis well designed to seduce Louis Philippe's adversaries, and to throw discredit on that law of exile whose repeal would immediately have authorised the Bonapartes, including the head of the family, to establish themselves in Paris – in other words in the very heart of the fray. 'If France goes on rejecting us, I am sorry for France,' he went on, 'she is repelling those of her children who are most devoted to her glory, her honour, her liberty – children who owe her so much that they are ready for all sorts of sacrifices and will devote the rest of their days to her, convinced that they can serve their country in any post.* If King Jérôme is to be believed, the republicans were ready to come to terms so as to bring down the July Monarchy, and were planning to send two of their number, Cavaignac and Bastide, to London towards the end of 1832, with the mission of reaching an understanding with the ex-King of Spain.

Louis Philippe and his ministers ignored these dangerous declarations, and the law of April 1832, confirming their banishment, reduced the hopes of the clan to nought. Much put out, Joseph had to make arrangements to settle definitely in London, though in fact it suited neither his temperament nor his health. His brothers Jérôme and Lucien visited him there, and he went with the latter as a tourist to Scotland: it did not take Prince Louis

---

* Joseph Bonaparte: *Lettres d'exil.*

long to realise that this sexagenarian uncle was not a serious rival, and to pose a second time as claimant.* The French government could expect audacious moves of every sort from him, and it was essential to foil them because the first incident might well unite, for the worse, legitimists, Bonapartists and republicans – for Queen Hortense's son was not afraid of the word republic, and partisans of Charles X were ready to combine with anyone in order to get rid of Louis Philippe.

Chateaubriand, emerging from seclusion during the July Monarchy, carried his disappointment to Switzerland, where he spoke and wrote about nothing but his fidelity to his oaths, tearfully remembering his king, the little Duc de Bordeaux, who was living humbly enough with his ancestor in the gloomy palace of Edinburgh, 'fallen from an eminence centuries old'. He paid court to Queen Hortense, however, 'whom war had created and the sword had defeated'; appraised Prince Louis as 'a well-educated young man, honourable and naturally serious'; froze with horror when he penetrated a closet filled with Bonaparte's effects, and went back to Lucerne to find Madame de Chateaubriand, who was following him like a faithful dog on a leash, grumbling about that Bonaparte family 'who can't realise that they signify nothing'. However, between that nothingness and the Orleanist usurper his choice was now made, and a few weeks later he wrote to Hortense's son who had sent him a pamphlet called *Political Musings*: 'You know, Prince, that my young king is in Scotland, and that so long as he lives there can be no other king of France for me but him; yet if God, in his impenetrable wisdom, had rejected the race of Saint Louis, if the customs of our country made a republican state possible, there is no name to suit the glory of France better than your own.'

This is one of the themes of his manifesto: *Of the new proposition concerning the banishment of Charles X and his family*, in the

* It was during Lucien's visit in July 1833 that the two brothers published their Manifesto 'Of the Consular or Imperial Republic', which attracted very little notice.

course of which, with a certain nobility he took upon himself to defend Napoleon's son: 'What history conferred on the Duc de Bordeaux, the Duke of Reichstadt drew from his father's fame. Napoleon advanced more rapidly than lineage: taking long strides, ten years were enough for him to put whole centuries behind him. For religious men, and those dominated by the prejudice of blood, the Duke of Reichstadt was a figure who accorded with their ideas: consecrated by the Pope himself, ennobled by a daughter of the Caesars. As I have said elsewhere: his mother gave him the past, his father the future. In France there were still many generations who by recognising Napoleon II would only have returned to the fidelity they swore to Napoleon I. The army would have been proud to receive the descendant of his victories.'

*   *   *

The new King of the French, a foxy politician, did his best to outwit all these apologists by giving the cult of the Emperor the constitutional government's guarantee and patronage. He went in person to the inauguration ceremony of the statue on the Vendôme column, and may well have smiled inwardly as he read the commemorative inscription: 'July 28, 1833, anniversary of the July Revolution, and the third year of the reign of Louis Philippe I, King of the French, by royal command of July 8, 1831, on the suggestion of M. Casimir Périer, the statue of Napoleon on the column of the Grande Armée has been replaced, M. Thiers being Minister of Public Works'.* When the veil fell, and the silhouette haunting so many people's memories was outlined against the sky, the King raised his plumed cocked hat and gave the signal for rejoicing by crying out 'Long live the Emperor!' It was much too

---

* The first statue, the work of Chaudet in 1810, represented the Emperor in Roman dress. That of 1833, by Seurre cast by Crozatier (now in the Invalides after having been thrown to the ground in 1871) represented him wrapped in the famous grey overcoat. The present statue, signed by Dumont, is a reproduction of Chaudet's.

glib a gesture, and the factions sneered, and accused royalty and the royalist party of 'hanging on to the grey overcoat', of 'misrepresenting Napoleon by their glorification' after betraying and insulting him. King Joseph was the first to take umbrage over this annexation, and seized pen and ink to make a further attack on the law which frustrated his plans: 'France has set up *his* statue, but his family are still banished, though their crimes are merely that they have inherited Napoleon's name.' In January 1834 this provoked a petition from a man called Girardet 'with a view to reopening French territory to all members of the Bonaparte family': the Chamber reacted suspiciously and passed on to the order of the day, refusing to hear him. Then Lucien joined his brother in a firm protest to Marshal Soult, Louis Philippe's Foreign Secretary; it was unsuccessful but some members of the Assembly and Méneval (Napoleon's secretary, who listened to all back-stairs rumours) led them to believe that the affair would be raised in the next session, that there was talk of proposing an amendment allowing the women to return at once and leaving the King to decide personally as to the rest. 'The general opinion is that, for different motives, the members of the Emperor's family have been placed in a truly irregular situation.'

Nothing came of it however, and Joseph grew tired of these rebuffs, and in 1835 set off once more for the United States which he now called 'his second native land', leaving the ground open to the enterprises of his turbulent nephew, who paid no heed to the wise advice given him freely by Madame Mère. Moreover, the grandmother would not be there to lecture and guide this divided, scattered family much longer: she was dying, just at the moment when the battle to have the will from St. Helena executed was coming to a head, and in particular the question of the disposal of the objects intended for the Duke of Reichstadt, a subject that raised difficulties and excited ill-feeling.

According to British law, the original document had been deposited at the Prerogative Court of the Archbishopric of Canterbury on December 10, 1821, but probate had not been granted until August 1824. Meanwhile the executors had submitted a copy to the civil court in Paris, which entrenched itself behind the argument that Napoleon Bonaparte had been unable to make a valid will, since he had been subject to 'civil death'. Then Laffitte, the Emperor's chief banker, admitted that he owed the sum of 3,418,785 francs – which he considered not as an investment but as a deposit producing very low interest – but quibbled over the value of Montholon's proxy out of fear of Marie-Louise's claims, and in a word made a thousand difficulties to delay the restitution of a hoard which was bearing fruit inside his bank. It had been necessary to refer the matter to the courts to get the capital transferred to the Deposit and Consignment Office, whereupon the ex-Empress, having got wind of the controversy, put herself forward as heiress until 1826, on which date she had been discouraged by Charles X's government, instigated by Chateaubriand, Minister for Foreign Affairs. A court of arbitration, composed of Caulaincourt, former Master of the Horse, Maret and Daru, former ministerial secretaries, had divided Laffitte's funds between Montholon – who received the lion's share with more than a million – Bertrand and Marchand – each of whom had to make do with about 250,000 francs – and the Longwood domestics. Montholon, always unlucky or imprudent where business was concerned, had been waiting for this bonus to pay off his creditors. Major Jackson, who had been on Lowe's staff at St. Helena and very intimate with Montholon at that time, visited Frémigny in 1828 and was struck by the sumptuous anglomania reigning there: servants, horses and carriages all came from London and the lord of the manor kept open house. As Marie-Louise refused to return the two millions taken to Orleans in 1814, and Prince Eugène affirmed that he had honoured the notes drawn at St. Helena, thus cancelling his debt to his stepfather's executors, it had not been possible to carry out the codicils.

When Napoleon's son reached his sixteenth year in 1827, the executors had tried to go to Vienna to hand over his legacies to

him, remembrances of a father 'who would be the talk of the
entire universe', but they were firmly refused admittance and the
recluse in the Hofburg never received the sword from Austerlitz,
nor the gold dressing-case used at all the great battles, nor even
the camp-bed of his death agony at Longwood. General Bertrand,
who claimed to have been authorised by Napoleon to keep the
objects deposited with him in case of the death of the Duke of
Reichstadt, received an icy reprimand when he tried to exercise
that right in 1832: 'I hope they will not resort to violence,'
Madame Mère wrote to him 'and replace justice by force. However,
the matter is in your hands and you will not allow this important
bequest to pass into other hands than mine.'* On January 26,
several days before her death, the old lady once again pressed her
cousin, Arrighi de Casanova, to hasten the process of collecting
together the relics she wished to dispose of in her will: she was
never granted this ultimate satisfaction because on February 2 she
was laid in the ground, in the midst of the joyful cries of the
Roman Carnival. The news of her death moved Stendhal in his
consulate at Civita-Vecchia. 'What a fine character,' he notes in his
journal, 'where is there a queen in Europe with such a high moral
sense? . . . Hers was a soul worthy of Plutarch – that is to say as
different as possible from that of an ordinary princess.'

It was in this climate of revived fervour that in 1833 Antommarchi carried out a profitable operation by selling casts of his
death-mask of Napoleon on subscription, and this in spite of the
disappointment of some who found it did not correspond to the
criteria of phrenology, a science then in fashion: there was no
trace, they said, of 'bumps of genius', and Anatole France was
one of the first to suspect the Corsican doctor ('a garrulous,
hungry, stage apothecary') of having taken everyone in. In fact
it seemed, all considered, that if the central part of the mask had

* In October 1837 Bertrand was to publish a justification of his decision, which
is not altogether convincing.

In 1847 the son of King Jérôme exchanged a subacid correspondence with
Noverraz, former footman at Longwood, who refused to give up the objects
entrusted to him without an official receipt from *all* the Bonapartes.

really been cast from the corpse, the peripheral features – forehead, chin, neck, had been modelled afterwards. Hence the
unexpected result, but Bertrand, most faithful of the faithful,
owned one of the first examples, and his silence was in itself a sign
of approval, as was that of Marchand, Noverraz and Pierron, who
had all looked after the dying man and laid out the corpse.
Bertrand's mask, today in the collection of Prince Napoleon, bears
a dedication to the Countess Bertrand in Italian: 'To the incomparable merit of Madame Bertrand. August 27, 1821'. On any
possible construction, the inscription seems to be a reminder that
the Countess had had the audacity to take possession of the
mould (made by the English Dr. Burton) which Antommarchi
was eager to own so as to claim authorship of it.

To advertise his enterprise the doctor cleverly raised the
question of the return of Napoleon's remains, and addressed
himself directly to Louis Philippe, saying with his usual aplomb
that England 'was amazed to be the possessor of these French
ashes'.

V

A BONAPARTIST PRETENDER

*

Now that his uncle, King Joseph, had returned to the United States, and his father, King Louis, had chosen to live like a recluse in Florence, Prince Louis decided to act on his own: for the time had never been more favourable to his plans, and even Guizot – hardly to be suspected of sympathy for the pretender – was obliged to recognise the strength of the Bonapartist party, sustained by the inexhaustible capital represented by the very name of Napoleon: 'It's a great thing to be at the same time a national glory, a revolutionary guarantee and an authoritarian principle. Therein lies enough to survive great faults and long set-backs.'

Balzac, royalist and legitimist though he was, published in 1833 *Le Médecin de campagne*, a monument to the glory of the people's Napoleon.

'A sergeant, and even a private, could say "My Emperor" to him, just as you sometimes say to me "My good friend",' announces the infantryman Goguelat in a barn in Dauphiné.

In fact the ghost of Napoleon haunts the whole of *La Comédie Humaine*.* In *La Cousine-Bette* the beautiful Madame Hulot refuses the sovereign's homage. In *La femme de trente ans*, the action takes place on a Sunday, the thirteenth of the year 1813, before the army leaves for a military tattoo. The clock strikes one. Utter silence. Sound of spurs and the clink of swords. Napoleon is making a halt and the gentle Julie de Chatillonest immediately feels jealous of her lover, Colonel Victor d'Aiglemont, who has no

---

* In *Modeste Mignon*, published in 1844, Balzac went so far as to declare: 'There cannot be anything great in a century prefaced by Napoleon's reign.'

eyes for anyone but his Emperor. 'There was something pretar-
natural about him, a magic, a counterfeit of divine power, or
rather a fugitive image of a reign itself so fugitive ... Amid all the
outburst of enthusiasm at his presence, not a muscle of his face
seemed to move.'

'Oh, good God yes,' says a good-natured but conceited
grenadier. 'At Wagram in the thick of the firing, at the river
Moskva among the dead, always cool as a cucumber – *he* is.'

Balzac knew every feature of the 'pale and terrible caesarian
figure' from the accounts of the woman he was in love with in
1825, Laure Permon, Duchesse d'Abrantès. She was fifteen
years older than him. 'That woman,' he said proudly, 'saw
Napoleon as a child, she saw him as a young man, she saw him
occupied with everyday tasks; then she saw him grow great, rise
to fame and cover the world with his name. She is for me like a
blessèd spirit who has come to it beside me after living in heaven,
close to God.' In Laure d'Abrantès' house Balzac met Madame
Hamelin – 'la Merveilleuse' of 1796, the egeria of the mighty ones
of the Directory, by 1829 a quinquagenerian fond of brooding
over the past – Madame Récamier and the Princess Bagration,
widow of the Russian hero of Borodino. And on the bookcase in
his study, in a place of honour, he had placed a statuette of
Napoleon, with a paper band stuck to the pedestal bearing the
proud boast: 'What he could not achieve with his sword, I will
accomplish with my pen. Honoré de Balzac.'

The same year saw the publication of a collection of Béranger's
verse dedicated to his one time patron, Lucien Bonaparte, with a
preface referring reticently to 'the increasing despotism of the
Empire', while being impregnated with the author's enthusiastic
and faithful admiration 'for the Emperor's genius'. He declared
in no uncertain terms that this is not a political move, but admitted
that Napoleon's life was at that time a daily inspiration to him, and
'the greatest poem that the world ever had to admire'. As we have
already remarked, Béranger has often been suspected of oppor-
tunism, and it is true that his Bonapartist songs appeared

somewhat late in the day, but this didn't worry the people who sang them.

At Milan, in January 1818, Stendhal began on a *Life of Napoleon*, but he put the manuscript on one side and as his earlier works on Italian painting, Haydn or Mozart, did not give him the opportunity to express his views of politics, one must look in his *Journal* to find a confession of disillusion bordering on rage. The end of the epic had been 'heart-breaking', and Napoleon's downfall a true reverse of fortune. 'I fall with him,' he notes, before predicting: 'Everything that happens in France from now on should bear the epitaph: To the extinguisher.' Settled in Italy since 1815 to get away from France, and subject to crushing melancholy and loneliness, he says bitterly that the conquerors of the Empire have learnt nothing and forgotten nothing, and that they are trying to impose the social and religious politics of another century – just as if the French Revolution were a dead-letter. The feebleness and shilly-shallying of Louis XVIII's ministers were as intolerable to him as the retrograde ferocity of the Piedmontese monarchy, and he comments delightedly that 'the French are regretted at Naples as everywhere else. The best recommendations for a foreigner in Italy is to be a Frenchman attached to Napoleon's government'. He wrote later about Napoleon's activity in Italy: 'May 14, 1796, is an important date in the history of the human spirit. General-in-Chief Buonaparte entered Milan; Italy awoke, and for the historian of the human spirit, Italy will always be half of Europe.'

His impressions in London, where he stayed in 1817, were the same: 'Napoleon everywhere. If they had had a Napoleon themselves, they wouldn't say three words without mentioning him; we wouldn't be held worthy of untying their shoe-laces.'

What satisfaction, amid this grey bitterness, to dwell on thoughts of the lonely hero, to magnify the man of steel, the logician of action, 'the professor of energy': Stendhal's enthusiasm drove him to concentrate studiously on a historian's metier, with its rules and accuracy so foreign to his nature. Yet is not Napoleon the most Stendhalian of characters? – coldly allotting shares to reason and passion, cynical and solitary, constantly forced to gamble, if not to cheat, and who could himself have reflected, like Julien Sorel: 'In future I shall only count on those elements in my character which I have tested.'

In 1829 he conceived the idea for the novel *Le Rouge et le Noir*, a chronicle of the society of those conquered in 1815, the rise and fall of a young man born for an outstanding career under fire, and who was driven by defeat to assume the black dress of a priest, mourning for his lost illusions. Julien, 'crazy for a soldier's life', has to make do with the *Mémorial* for his bedside book: fiercely ambitious, cautious and calculating, plebeian, under the Empire he would have been a colonel at thirty; instead of that, the disappearance of his idol condemns him to a slow, painful and humiliating advancement in the morose society of the Restoration, to loneliness in a world of middle-class customs and conventions, his sole guide the memory that Bonaparte, 'an obscure and penniless lieutenant', had 'made himself master of the world with his sword'. The end of this strange 'preparation for misfortune' is the shooting of Madame de Rénal, prison, the idea of committing suicide and the final burst of Napoleonic pride: 'Kill myself! My God, no, Napoleon lived.'

Towards the end of 1836, when on leave in France, from his consulate at Civita-Vecchia, Stendhal put aside his manuscripts of *Lucien Leuwen* and *Vie de Henri Brulard* and began his *Mémoires sur Napoléon*, which occupied him until April 1837. The preface set the tone: 'The more of the whole truth is known, the greater Napoleon will become.' The populace judge a hero with their hearts; posterity has to confirm their judgement. A writer of the future may produce a meticulous study of the modern conqueror, but he will not have had the advantage of witnessing Napoleon's entry into Berlin in 1806, of seeing him toiling, stick in hand, in the retreat from Moscow or addressing the Council of State. Yet Beyle, remembering with satisfaction his own service in the Sixth Dragoons in Italy, and in the Commissariat des Guerres, his campaigns, Prussia, Wagram, Russia and Silesia, concluded coolly – when he no longer had to fear the wrath of the instigators of the Restoration – 'Love for Napoleon is the only passion that has remained to me.' It is known that he wished to have engraved on his tombstone an epitaph ending 'He respected one man alone: Napoleon'.

The work did not see the light until 1854, for Stendhal grew tired of the research necessary to a historical study, and abandoned his manuscript, to write *La Chartreuse de Parme* in fifty-two days, from November 4 to December 25, 1838 – a book whose hero, Fabrice del Dongo, like Julien Sorel and the author himself, is haunted by the already legendary personage. We see this in the first lines: 'On May 15, 1796, General Bonaparte entered Milan at the head of that youthful army which had just crossed the bridge of Lodi and taught the world that after so many centuries Caesar and Alexander had a successor.' Fabrice 'who thinks the middle classes ridiculous', disguised himself as a hussar so as to join the battle in the wake of his idol, arrives in the neighbourhood of Waterloo on the morning of June 18, 1815, without even knowing how to open a cartridge-case, gazes 'lost in childish admiration at the famous Prince of the Moskova, the bravest of the brave', and sees the Emperor go by in the middle of a group of gold-braided uniforms. The battle is lost, alas, and Fabrice frustrated of military glory leaves for Italy where he launches into a conflict between human ambitions, hiding the secret wound of his regret under the mask of a misanthrope, and going in solitary pursuit of a difficult happiness: an iron will, an energetic and well-balanced character, quick-witted and in control of himself – modelled on the man Stendhal had seen with his own eyes during the best years of his youth.

In 1835 it was the turn of Thiers to call to mind the grandeur and glories of the Empire, in his speech on reception into the Académie Française.

Louis Marchand published at Strasburg the text of the *Guerres de César*, followed by *Notes sur le deuxième livre de l'Enéide de*

Virgile, Observations sur la tragédie de Mahomet par Voltaire,
Note sur la suicide and *Deuxième codicile,* all taken down from
Napoleon's dictation at St. Helena. In his Preface, the Emperor's
executor announced the appearance of his own *Souvenirs*: 'They
come from memories in my heart which will never leave me. May
their publication some day show the Emperor as I saw him: great
in genius, talent and glory on the throne, great in courage and
resignation in adversity.'

Edgar Quinet, republican, published his ode, *Napoleon*, in
which the Emperor appears as a majestic hero 'in that sublime,
eternally serene and popular region where such figures as Prometheus, and Achilles are to be found, great leaders who dominate
human imagination'.* Enthusiasm luckily made up for lack of
poetic skill in such appeals as:

> 'Ecoute-moi, désert de'Asie
> T'en souviens-tu de ce lion,
> Effroi des lions de Syrie
> Qui s'appelait Napoléon?'

or prophecies like:

> 'Il n'est pas mort! Il n'est pas mort!
>   De son sommeil
> Le géant va sortir, plus grand à son reveil.'

The painter Horace Vernet exhibited large canvases on the
subject of Jena, Friedland, Wagram, and in July 1836 the inauguration of the Arc de Triomphe gave old memories new life.
It was in vain for Louis XVIII to decree in 1823 that the monument commemorated the glory of the Duc d'Angoulême, and

---

* There were some discordant notes in the concert however – Auguste Barbier,
for instance, wrote angrily:
> 'Ainsi passez, passez monarques, débonnaires
> Doux pasteurs de l'humanité.
> Passez, passez, pour vous point de haute statue
> Le peuple perdra votre nom.
> Car il ne se souvient que de l'homme qui tue
> Avec le sabre et le canon.'

later for Louis Philippe to announce that it celebrated the military
glory of the Republic and the Empire – after dedicating a gallery
at Versailles to the chief Napoleonic victories – the others, namely
the old men, the poets and soldiers, associated it with the feats of
the Emperor's armies and Victor Hugo spoke for them when he
wrote:

> 'O vaste entassement ciselé par l'histoire
> Monceau de pierre assis sur un monceau de gloire.'

Next year, in his *Servitude et grandeur-militaires*, Vigny
resuscitated his dreams as a schoolboy under the Empire, and
described the days 'when logarithms and tropes were in our eyes
no more than steps to climb to the star of the Legion of Honour,
to children the loveliest star in the sky'. He too had been born too
late to gain glory in the military profession: so he retired into
solitude and expressed his regrets in frigidly beautiful alexandrines.
His *Capitaine Renaud*, an incarnation of 'the education of a great
soul by harsh circumstances', comes straight out of the gallery of
military 'martyrs to honour': in Egypt at the age of twelve this
brave fellow found himself in the presence of General Bonaparte
and experienced a shock which had a decisive effect on his
existence: 'My head span, I felt that he was my master, who was
carrying away my soul ... I felt as afraid as Moses, when as a
shepherd he saw God in the burning bush. Bonaparte had lifted
me up a free man, and when his arms gently let me down again
on to the bridge, he left one slave more there.'

In February of the same year, Musset had published his
Confession d'un enfant du siècle, wherein he brings to life those
adolescents who are 'visited by their fathers between two battles,
and who spend their schooldays to the rattle of drums'. This
account of the poet's love affair with George Sand reflects the
generation who heard the stone fall on the grave at St. Helena and
saw 'the glacial star of reason' ascend the skies, 'shedding light
without warmth, enveloping the world, in a livid shroud'. An
empty life, a grey horizon. 'Enter the priesthood', they say to
those who dream of glory, to the ambitious, enthusiastic or

generous. Disgust with life, the melancholy of young creatures born too late for the brilliant life of camps, whose apprenticeship to misfortune is served in the ruins of their illusions. Stendhal was soon to make Lucien Leuwen say: 'I respect Washington, but he bores me, whereas young General Bonaparte, the conqueror of the bridge of Arcole, thrills me more than the finest pages of Homer and Tasso'.

So here we have Napoleon, the forceful politician *par excellence*, as the hero of a romantic movement, bearer of the message of freedom of language and ideas . . . The choice is not paradoxical: the young Bonaparte brought up in the patriarchal decor of Corsica, the poor but ambitious officer, the brilliant victories of Egypt and Italy at the head of an army which broke the chains of servitude and spoke only of emancipation, compelled the admiration of the new poets who set heroism in the front rank of the virtues. The Empire was thus equated with the man who subjugated Fate, and St. Helena was an apotheosis unequalled in Romanticism.

All this had eclipsed the Duc d'Angoulême's 'glory', and relegated the hard-won Algerian victories to an inferior plane (although it was there that the young Duc d'Orléans distinguished himself), while the French people, hungry for noble deeds, were all the more infatuated by the recent past because the present seemed so grey and unpromising. In 1831 there had been a revolt of the silk-weavers of Lyons, and in 1834 several risings in Paris: even Béranger, cautious as he was by nature, was not afraid to think that the government had been unable to resolve social problems. 'A new order, different from the old, is struggling to be born,' he wrote. 'In spite of the clumsiness of the midwives, the birth will take place.' And in 1835, the prudent, bourgeois monarchy suffered a rude shock: Fieschi's infernal machine celebrated the anniversary of the days of July 1830 in revolutionary style . . .

This was the moment to dream of the man who had made glory everybody's daily bread ; such dreams are a drug helping people to forget their poverty and financial struggles; but though poetry, engravings and songs combined to call to mind all that was inspired and exceptional in the personality of Napoleon, intoxicating in his vision, touching in the death of his son in exile in the flower of his youth, they did not help fathom the problem of Bonapartism, of succession, of dynasty. As Chateaubriand put it, the death at St. Helena 'closed the era of the past'. Few people knew that a pretender existed in the person of the son of the ex-King of Holland. The Emperor's nephew? Did he have brothers then? How far away it all seemed and how quickly people forgot everyone who did not shine as *He* did with such exceptional brilliance.*

They were to be caught unawares on October 30, 1836 . . .

* * *

At six o'clock on the morning of that day, a strange scene was played out at Strasburg, in the courtyard of the Austerlitz barracks. 'Fall in' had sounded and the soldiers of the fourth regiment of artillery formed in a square – this had been General Bonaparte's regiment during the siege of Toulon and had distinguished itself after Napoleon's return from Elba by offering him the keys to the town of Grenoble. Their colonel, Vaudrey, a veteran of the Russian and Waterloo campaigns, hurried to meet a little group of riders and saluted them respectfully: in the grey light of dawn he was the only man who recognised Prince Louis Napoleon, arrived from Switzerland the evening before and wearing the uniform of a lieutenant of artillery. With him was Parquin, whose wife was reader to Queen Hortense, in the uniform of a brigadier-general, another man in that of a major, and several officers of the garrison who were in the plot. Drawing his sword, he declared:

---

* Béranger himself (and no one could tax him with Bonapartism) said haughtily in 1833: 'Louis Philippe is the king France needs. Napoleon was an isolated phenomenon.'

'Soldiers, a revolution has taken place. The Empire is re-established. We no longer have a bourgeois king reigning in Paris, but a new emperor, a new Napoleon.'

The Prince came forward and in a solemn voice with a slight German accent began to speak about glory and victory. Someone brandished the eagle of the fifth regiment of infantry; it was the same that had greeted the Emperor at Laffrey in 1815.

'Let us swear to be faithful to the eagle of the great Napoleon!' said the pretender.

There were cries of 'Long live the Emperor!' and then the regiment lined up and followed the Prince through the streets of the sleeping town in the direction of the infantry barracks, while a message was dispatched to the address of Queen Hortense, announcing: 'I am marching on Paris. Louis.' Alas, although the prefect was surprised in his dressing-gown and taken away cursing and well-guarded, the town-major quickly succeeded in gathering a regiment and turning the situation to his advantage: after a few blows had been exchanged between artillery and infantry, the Prince was seized, shut up in the fortress and later in the town prison.

Paris was in a state of uneasiness all that night, because the dispatch sent from Strasburg, mutilated by bad weather, arrived in a menacingly laconic form: 'This morning at about six o'clock Louis Napoleon, son of the Duchesse de Saint-Leu, with the connivance of Colonel Vaudrey of the artillery, rode through the streets of Strasburg with a party of . . .' The cabinet gathered at the Tuileries and sat up to wait for a courier who didn't come. Queen Amélie and the young princes were infected by the general panic – the Duc d'Orléans talked of going immediately to Strasburg – and the King seemed crushed. He had his reasons: a republican insurrection at Lyons in 1834, seven plots to assassinate him between the autumn of 1834 and the summer of 1835, and finally Fieschi's attempt in July 1835 had filled him with gloom, and he took this new threat very badly. Of course Prince Louis was a young man quite unknown in France, and had never achieved anything except publish his *Rêveries politiques* and a *Projet de constitution* but had he not the prestige of his name? The old king would have been more afraid if he had known what strength animated this dreamer and what faith he had in his destiny!

In the small hours an aide-de-camp to the general in command at Strasburg at last arrived, with an account of what proved to be merely an abortive attempt: both the prefect and the commanding officer had regained their liberty, and all the conspirators, with the exception of Persigny who had escaped were under lock and key.

This pathetic dénouement discredited the pretender and left the Bonapartists crestfallen, whereas Louis Philippe, greatly reassured, decided to play the benevolent monarch. The Prince embarked on the *Andromède*, after being provided by the sub-prefect of Lorient with a viaticum of 15,000 francs, and travelled to the United States to gather strength for a fresh *coup*; when his confederates appeared at the assizes they were acquitted, with applause from those present.

Guizot was indignant at this royal benevolence: 'I am inclined to think that such striking complaisance on the part of the constitutional government of 1830 towards national memories and popular sentiments that are hardly in tune with its liberal and pacific policy, was going beyond what was necessary, I would even say suitable.' Perhaps Louis Philippe was more perspicacious than his minister, but he was well aware that a section of public opinion approved of his moderation. The escapade unloosed the sarcasms of the press, but it had also shown France that a pretender to the throne existed whose audacity was reminiscent of his uncle's, and Metternich, who had already summed him up, put the French ambassador on his guard with the foresight of a real statesman:

'Take care, this young fool has gained importance from your misguided habit of exalting everything to do with the Emperor Napoleon to an exaggerated extent. You'll end by making people believe in the future of a Napoleonic dynasty.'

Lamartine, who thought the pretender should be banished for life, expressed the same fears in 1837 when he warned deputies against the attraction inherent in the name of Napoleon: 'a name which has too much brilliance, which still echoes too resoundingly in certain ears for the good of the country.' Stendhal was not the man to contradict him. Finding himself at the fair of Beaucaire in July of that same year, and venturing into the tent of a mountebank exhibiting wax figures of famous men, he noticed with delight that in a corner where Napoleon lay stretched on his death-bed a religious silence reigned, broken by one of the mountebanks brandishing a kerchief which he claimed had belonged to the illustrious exile of St. Helena and which could be touched for two sous. 'Gentlemen,' said he, 'this is my own property; but don't give me anything unless you want to, you aren't obliged to.'

VI

MONSIEUR THIERS' GREAT PLAN

✳

In 1839 a pamphlet was published in Paris by Paulin: its title was *Idées Napoléoniennes* and its author was Prince Louis, who used often to maintain to his friends:

'It's not only the Emperor's ashes, but his ideas which need shifting.'

He had left America at the end of 1837 and hurried to Arenenberg to receive his mother's last wishes; then he settled in London, in September 1838, after his presence in Switzerland had brought France and the Confederation to the brink of the battlefield. France had used diplomatic channels to ask for the Prince to be expelled from Swiss territory. The Canton of Thurgau remained adamant. The French government sent 20,000 men to the frontier and Berne mobilised her army. With considerable dignity, Prince Louis put an end to the difference by voluntarily leaving Switzerland for England. There he lived very modestly, sometimes borrowing money, but spending it only on propaganda with the firm determination of a man who has a rendezvous with destiny.

'The Napoleonian theory is not a warlike one,' he emphasised, 'but social, industrial, commercial and humane.'

When so many others were intoxicated by their memories of conquests and glory, this astute young man kept his head and decided that it would be more effective, and so more profitable, to present the founder of his dynasty under the seductive aspect of a social reformer. There was one man at least who did not fall into the trap – that was the crafty, subtle Thiers, who always thought of Queen Hortense's son as 'a little Swiss with something

German about him'. The poor man would have been astounded
had he been told in 1840 that the establishment of the Empire
would force him to undertake countless transformations, the most
ironical being support of the Orleanist cause . . . At that period the
young Bonaparte and the Marseillais statesman were men of the
future, as they both knew: one preparing to disembark at
Boulogne from London, the other delighted to occupy the chair
of the President of the Council, just abandoned by Marshal Soult,
Duc de Dalmatie. It would be impossible to imagine two more
dissimilar characters. One, the heir to a name worth several armies,
who advanced as one of his friends said 'preceded by his shadow',
but whose dreams were ambitious, who saw far ahead and
murmured with confident amiability: 'Everything happens in the
end; one must be prepared for everything.' The other a turbulent
barrister from the south, 'a quick-silver character', Balzac's
Rastignac, who meddled in everything and desired everything,
whether in politics or literature, with the keenness of a true
bourgeois. But they had one passion in common: in 1837 Thiers
told King Jérôme:

'Of all the Frenchmen of my day, I'm one of those most
attached to the glorious memory of Napoleon.'*

This statement was nothing but the truth, because after his
history of the Revolution, Thiers was now compiling another,
of the Consulate and Empire, and in the secrecy of his study he
cherished the as yet chimeric hope of associating his name to
displays which would thrill the nation, and his government with
a step that would dismiss into the background all parliamentary
squabbles, public discontent, and the sulky hostility of Louis
Philippe, who was dreaming of having Monsieur Guizot captain-
ing the ship of state.

It has been suggested that the government had got wind of one
project of Napoleon's brothers, who were plotting to get England

* 'Since M. Thiers planned to write a history of Napoleon,' jeered Alphonse
Karr, 'and has written his name on the boots of the bronze statue in the Place
Vendôme, he identifies himself with that personage in the most extraordinary way.'

to give back the illustrious exile's remains, and that 'grouped around his glorious coffin, they would defy the laws of banishment, and return to France'; or perhaps that the Irish M.P., Daniel O'Connell, egged on by Prince Louis, would put the same project before the London House of Commons with the embarrassing result of forcing the Foreign Secretary to state publicly that England was prepared to give up the ashes on condition that France would ask for them . . . It seems that the determining factor was actually the tenacity of Monsieur Thiers, spurred on by his feelings as a historian, and convinced (as a good statesman) that he would be giving satisfaction to those who were behind both social unrest and the rebuffs the country was receiving in the Middle East, and who delightedly repeated Lamartine's comment: 'France is bored.' There had been 64 strikes in 1839 and 130 in 1840. At the Tuileries there was considerable dread of a movement of what was called 'the working classes'. In the Middle East, Mehemet Ali, protected by France, was threatened by an agreement between England, Prussia and Russia, with the object of forcing him to submit to the Sultan of Turkey, who was protected by London. Such a triumphal return would raise the prestige of the bourgeois régime and establish the July monarchy as a national system.

It was an attractive proposition, but a ticklish one, and Louis Philippe – no longer the king of the barricades but an authoritarian seventy-year-old – took a lot of persuading: he felt that the resurrection of the conqueror would show up in a painful light the humiliation he himself had been imposing on the country ever since 1830, to guarantee peace and make his régime secure. To protect the economy on which the future of his régime depended, Louis Philippe had refused French aid to the Polish Revolution in 1830, declined the crown of Belgium offered to the Duc de Nemours in 1831, put a brake on the conquest of Algeria, and given way to England in the Middle East.

He thought he had done enough for the people's religion by restoring the statue to the Place Vendôme, completing the Arc

The embarkation of Napoleon's body at St. Helena

The transhipment of Napoleon's coffin from *La Belle-Poule* to the *Normandie* at Cherbourg

de Triomphe 'to the glory of the French armies', and installing portraits of the Emperor and pictures of his victories at Versailles, but in order to satisfy one party and win over the other (the Bonapartists) it was well worth celebrating a mass at the Invalides, and he gave way.

When receiving the allegiance of his ministers on May 1, 1840, St. Philip's day, he announced cheerfully to Thiers:

'I am giving you a present for my name-day. You wish to bring back Napoleon's remains to France. I consent. Come to an agreement on the subject with the British government. We will send Joinville to St. Helena.' He had said privately to the Austrian ambassador Apponyi: 'Sooner or later this would have been forced on me by petitions ... I prefer to grant it freely. There's no danger. The family is of no importance.'

Thiers was overjoyed, and at once opened the question with the British ambassador in Paris, not at all averse to going one better than his old enemy Guizot, who represented France in London. 'Monsieur Thiers yesterday officially stated to me the request of the French government that Her Majesty's Government should permit the transfer of the body of the late Emperor to Paris, observing that nothing would more tend to cement the union between the two nations and create a friendly feeling towards England in France than the aquiescence of the British government,' wrote the ambassador, Lord Granville.

That conservative champion of authoritarianism, Guizot, adviser to Louis XVIII during the Hundred Days, was one of those who had also enjoyed favour under the Empire: at the age of twenty-five, an unknown little provincial, he had been appointed professor of Modern History at the Sorbonne – though he possessed neither admiration nor even esteem for Napoleon. His expression was sour as he read Thiers' dispatch: 'The King agrees to transport Napoleon's remains from St. Helena to the Invalides. He approves of the idea as much as I do, and that is saying a great deal. The consent of the British Cabinet must therefore be obtained. I do not know any honourable motive for refusal ...

England cannot tell the world that she wishes to keep a corpse prisoner. When a condemned man has been executed, his body is returned to his family. But may Heaven pardon me for comparing the greatest of men to a criminal executed on the scaffold!'

A strange message, thought Guizot! Shouldn't this matter of the transport of his body be left to Napoleon's family? Could the King have forgotten the intrigues of Joseph Bonaparte and Prince Louis? Had he realised that the glorification of the Emperor's memory might appear as a provocation in Europe, and a weakness in his own country? 'To anyone of common sense,' he wrote in his *Mémoires*, 'crowds of objections present themselves. But there is generosity and majesty in the project.' He then drew up, but without great enthusiasm, the note that was sent to Lord Palmerston at the Foreign Office: 'The King has very much at heart a desire that Napoleon's body should lie in France, in that soil he defended and made illustrious, and which respectfully shelters the mortal remains of so many thousands of his companions in arms, both leaders and soldiers, who like him devoted their lives to serving their country. The undersigned feels sure that Her Britannic Majesty's government will see nothing in this desire of His Majesty the King of France but just and pious feelings, and will be eager to give the necessary orders so that Napoleon's body may be transported from St. Helena to France.' It wasn't the best Guizot, nor even the best diplomatic style . . .

Palmerston was neither romantic nor sentimental, and he was simply awaiting some move with regard to the tiresome affair in the Middle East: this talk of 'Bonaparte's' ashes produced a fleeting smile – 'What a very French démarche' he later confided to his brother with some amusement – but he made sure that the Queen's ambassador in Paris took Monsieur Thiers the favourable response evolved by the Cabinet the evening before: 'Her Majesty's Government hope that the readiness with which this answer is given will be looked upon in France as a proof of the desire of Her Majesty's government to obliterate every remnant of these national animosities which, during the life of the Emperor, assayed the French and English peoples in arms against each other, and Her Majesty's government trust that if any such feelings still continue anywhere they will be buried in the grave to which these remains are about to be consigned?'

Thiers was overjoyed, and went in person to thank the British ambassador, while the old Duke of Wellington, leader of the opposition, haughtily approved a decision which sealed such a spectacular reconciliation. These rejoicings were a little premature, for difficulties arose the very next day, which Lord Granville was at once begged to settle. At first, London insisted that the French ceremony should be organised with as little pomp as possible at St. Helena. 'Whatever measures are taken for the removal of Napoleon Bonaparte's remains, the proceedings of the Commissioner, while at St. Helena, should be conducted with as little display as possible and especially without any allusion or reference to the former situation of Napoleon Bonaparte as prisoner at St. Helena, in order to avoid anything that might possibly give rise to feelings of irritation in the minds of any portion of the British public.' (Palmerston to Granville, May 16, 1840. Unpublished.) Thiers promised that the French commissioner would be chosen personally by himself, and should be a member of the Ministry for Foreign Affairs and not one of the Emperor's companions at St. Helena, also that the latter should be instructed: 'to be silent and unemotional.' There would be no speeches, no demonstration, and anyone liable to create excitement, such as painters and writers, would be kept away. 'The excitement will be in France, *en famille*,' he explained to Guizot. The London government would not therefore be exposed to any outburst from the opposition, nor – more troublesome still – to the danger of a public justification of the illustrious prisoner's treatment.

Fortified by these assurances the British cabinet warned the governor of St. Helena, by the pen of Lord John Russell, the Colonial Secretary, to do nothing which might be interpreted as a denial or disavowal of the policy of 1815 towards the prisoner;

since the cabinet would see with lively displeasure any act, or any word which could give the Tories grounds or pretext to complain or protest. This was quite enough to make an official, faced with being involved with high diplomacy for a few weeks, cautious if not suspicious . . .

Suddenly a rumour went the rounds that quicklime had been put in the coffin in 1821. This had to be contradicted, and Sir Hudson Lowe's dispatch describing the funeral made public. However, Thiers got leave to authorise the French commissioner to get the coffin opened, in order to quash this report, and armed with Palmerston's dispatch to his ambassador in Paris, he insisted that the title of Emperor should be adopted in the official report of the exhumation and handing over of the body . . . It was a bitter blow, but the Secretary of State, who was busy preparing an agreement concerning Egyptian affairs with Austria, Prussia and Russia – but excluding France from what was an essentially European question – did not wish to poison relations with Paris, and therefore agreed to these few civilities.

*   *   *

On May 12, the Comte de Rémusat, Minister of the Interior, climbed the tribune of the Chamber of Deputies, in a state of ill-concealed emotion.

'Gentlemen, the King has instructed His Royal Highness Monseigneur the Prince de Joinville, to go with his frigate to the the island of St. Helena and bring back the mortal remains of the Emperor Napoleon (*Burst of applause*). We have come here to ask for the means of receiving them worthily on French soil. He was emperor and king, he was the legitimate sovereign of our country; as such he is entitled to be buried at Saint-Denis, but Napoleon must not have the usual burial of a king. He must continue to reign and command within the walls where the soldiers of our country lie, and where those who are called upon to defend her always go for inspiration.'

The minister's emotions was contagious: the deputies of both right and left rose to their feet, and cheered the government representative, who had stressed:

'The 1830 Monarchy is unique and the legitimate heir to all the memories of which France is justly proud. It is without doubt right for that monarchy, which was the first to rally all the forces and conciliate the desires of the French Revolution, to raise and honour fearlessly the statue and the tomb of the people's hero.'

Thiers had won his victory at last, although difficulties were not long in appearing: the Bonapartists were not content with a mere frigate, they wanted a whole squadron, others thought the Invalides unworthy and wanted the Vendôme column made into a mausoleum. The press became involved, spoke of 'national expiation' and blamed what they described as 'hypocritical reserve'. A Bonapartist news-sheet recalled 'the sublime agony of St. Helena, as full of resignation as that of Christ'. The enthusiasm reached the provinces: the town of Bourbon-Vendée wanted to return to its old name of Napoléon-Vendée. Rémusat having underlined Napoleon's 'legitimacy', there were some who maintained that this amounted to recognising King Joseph's right to 'the succession'. Were they to watch the pretender himself and the members of his family, follow the conqueror's coffin through a delirious Paris? Lamartine was dumbfounded and angry: 'Napoleon's ashes are not extinct and we are suffering from the sparks.' Guizot let himself be won over and entered the controversy: 'I'm for the Invalides, a military funeral, but religious and exemplary. Public places are impossible and unsuitable ... The Pantheon is common ground, profane and profaned. The Madeleine is a Greek tomb. Saint-Denis is for kings by profession. The Invalides alone is suited to the man and to his glory.'

The commission appointed to study the project listened to all this talk, insisted on the tribute of an equestrian statue, decided that the sum accredited was parsimonious, and on Marshal Clauzel's suggestion raised it to two million. In the Chamber of Deputies there was talk of the 'national hero'; even the republicans were carried away by phrases, images and memories, and declared without a smile that 'God had seemed astonished by Napoleon's superhuman genius'. This was the signal for Lamartine to rise to his feet in a rage, intending to pour water on this sacred fire, because a poet – in his words – sits above the battle, and willingly takes the national conscience upon himself. The painter Falconet watched him climb to the tribune, 'erect, firm, a little stiff. His forehead with its short greying hair bore the signs of thought strongly imprinted on his icy pallor, marbled with swelling blue veins ... His sonorous voice was blended with all the suppleness of rhythm; it vibrated with feeling, passion and indignation, and thundered with restrained energy, his deep tones echoing in every corner of the assembly:

'No, I do not love those men whose official doctrine is liberty, legality and progress, yet who take the sword and despotism for their symbols. Yes, I admit that I cannot understand it. I do not trust such contradictions. I am afraid lest that enigma may one day be explained and accepted. I would not have thought it a misfortune for Napoleon's memory if fate had left him for some time longer under the willow-tree at St. Helena ... Perhaps, for many reasons, those ashes have not yet cooled enough to be touched ... If that great general had been a great man in every sense, an irreproachable citizen, if he had been the Washington of Europe ... who knows if he would not sleep more peacefully, and perhaps more neglected, in his tomb.'*

'You are offending our country!' protested some deputies.

'No, gentlemen, I am merely describing human nature!'

Plain speaking came as a shock to men some of whom had been the Emperor's obedient servants.

'I do not hold with enthusiasm without recollection or foresight. I do not bow before that memory. I am not a member of the

---

* Lamartine detested Napoleon—that Caesar 'without heart or soul': sometimes he reproached him for not having avenged the Kings sometimes for 'having made himself a living reaction to the past'. Later on, while agreeing that 'liberty honours everyone but has never saved anyone', he even allowed himself to admire that excellent political brain, 'sublime reaction against anarchy'.

Napoleonic religion, of that cult of force which for some time
past this nation has attempted to substitute for the serious
religion of liberty ... Whether you choose Saint-Denis or the
Pantheon, or the Invalides, remember to inscribe on the monument
which commemorates him as soldier, consul, legislator and
emperor, the only inscription that expresses both your enthusiasm
and your prudence, the only inscription appropriate to that
unique man and the difficult epoch in which you are living: *To
Napoleon ... alone.*'

The generous-minded poet voted for the project, however,
and it was adopted by 280 votes to 65, but his speech incited the
House to reject the commission's suggestion of doubling the
initial allowance. There was an outcry in the press. The left-
wing papers slanged the government: 'So this is our national
recognition, marked down to the lowest price and included in the
budget,' was the line of *Le Siècle*. Another paper, *Le Courrier
français*, fulminated against this 'cut price' tomb. They were
indignant that the transfer of the ashes should cost less than the
expedition to Luxor and the erection of the obelisk in the Place
de la Concorde, whereas in London the Duke of Wellington's
victory had been commemorated both by a bridge and a statue.
The ultra-legitimist *Gazette de France* gave way to a vicious bout
of ill-temper at the news that 'Napoleon was to be glorified and
made a god of', and *Le National*, the opposition paper, feigned
indignation at the thought that they were going to 'violate the
sanctity of tombs, freeze at its source the poetry of misfortune,
and substitute the vulgar details of a burial to an apotheosis
gathered from memories'. Alphonse Karr wrote: 'This solitary
tomb on a rock battered by winds and sea had a grandeur that
could not be given it in Paris. At St. Helena, Napoleon was as far
from us and as deified as he would have been in heaven. People
go to Mecca to worship the tomb of Mahomet; it was to Jerusalem,
the site that witnessed his shameful execution, that Christians
went (when there were Christians) to adore Christ.' *Le Courrier
français*, *Le Constitutionel*, *Le Messager*, *Le Commerce* and *Le*

Siècle together started a subscription to raise the funds refused by
the deputies, but had to abandon it, so great was the fear that it
would constitute a serious criticism of the stinginess of parliament.

The law passed on June 6 ordered that the remains should be
taken to the Invalides. The Champ-de-Mars, the Madeleine, the
Pantheon, the Abbey of Saint-Denis, the Vendôme column and
the Place de la Bastille were all rejected in turn. 'At the Invalides
. . . he will still be in exile,' growled Alphonse Karr once more, 'it
is cowardice; they are afraid of upsetting the legitimist party.
Napoleon ought to be buried at Saint-Denis, among the kings and
the glorious ones of France, at Saint-Denis, where a few years ago I
saw the vault he destined for himself, with two enormous bronze
doors, executed according to his orders, to shut it.' It is true that
Napoleon had undertaken to arrange for a crypt for his dynasty in
the mausoleum of the kings of France, and that on April 26, 1821,
a few days before his death, he was still talking about his place of
burial: 'the Emperor wishes to be buried in the cemetery of
Père-Lachaise', Bertrand reported . . . 'but if the Bourbons put
him at Saint-Denis, that will be better still'. Heinrich Heine
rejoiced openly at the popular enthusiasm and replied sharply to
Lamartine: 'It is the man who represents young France confronted
by old Europe who is being glorified, for the French people
conquered and were humiliated and outraged in his person, and
in his person they are honouring, celebrating and rehabilitating
themselves.'

'Once the expedition was decided on,' wrote a witness, the
Abbé Coquereau, 'it was a question of who should take part . . .
Everyone wanted to see the famous rock, breathe the air of
Longwood, touch the earth of the grave and follow the mourning
procession throughout the four thousand leagues of the journey.'
One gallant fellow showed the twenty wounds he had received
when defending an eagle, another remembered being banished,
yet another recorded that he had been at Fontainebleau in 1814,
like General Petit, when the Emperor said goodbye to his army.
People were already anxious about the protocol of the religious

ceremony: 'They say they will sing a mass of Cherubini's, *the same* that was sung when Louis XVIII died,' noted Alphonse Karr. 'It would seem that they might have run to the expense of a new mass for Napoleon.'

The Prince de Joinville, twenty-two-year-old captain of *La Belle-Poule*, was to be at the head of this historic crusade, which would be followed from afar by the good wishes and prayers of all the Emperor's faithful friends, but a diplomat – Rohan-Chabot, Comte de Jarnac – son of one of the King's aides-de-camp and attached to the French embassy in London, was to be in charge of relations with the British authorities at St. Helena, under the title of King's Commissioner. According to Guizot: 'the choice of the Comte de Rohan-Chabot as Commissioner exactly suited the situation and the intentions of both cabinets. As whole-heartedly French as he was devoted to the King, and well-known in England where he had lived for some years as secretary to the French embassy, no one could be better fitted to go with Monseigneur the Prince de Joinville, whom his father the King had placed at the head of the expedition.' Louis Philippe's third son confessed later in his *souvenirs* that the mission of 'undertaker's mute' assigned to him did not please him overmuch. No doubt he envied his brothers, Aumale and Orléans, who were fighting in Algeria. He also disliked his name being associated with the return of the body of Bonaparte, usurper of the throne of his ancestors. It did not take him long to change his attitude, and decide that to bring back to France the ashes of 'this incomparable warrior whose genius had shed an immortal glow on our armies even in defeat', was in a way to raise aloft once more the standards of conquered France.

In response to the wish of the public, Thiers invited the survivors of the exile to take part in the glorious journey. Bertrand, former Grand Marshal of Longwood and a widower since 1836 living in retirement at Châteauroux, asked if he could take with him his son Arthur, born in exile in 1817, and presented by the Comtesse Bertrand to Napoleon as 'the first Frenchman who has entered the island without Hudson Lowe's permission'. Las Cases was blind and had only two years more to live; his place was taken by his son Emmanuel, the little copyist of the *Mémorial*, who had had the special honour of writing to the great man's dictation at St. Helena, and the courage to go to London to horse-whip the sinister Hudson Lowe. Gourgaud had become stout, red-faced and grey-haired, with a pointed beard, thick whiskers and heavy brows over bright eyes; at fifty-seven he had lost none of his pride and aggressiveness, and had enjoyed royal favour since 1830. First reinstated in his rank of brigadier, he afterwards commanded the garrison artillery in Paris and at Vincennes, was aide-de-camp to the King and commanded the artillery of the north, and after 1835 wore the epaulettes of a lieutenant-general. His having signed, in 1821, a petition asking for the return of the Emperor's remains was quite enough to make him arrogantly assume that the expedition was the fruit of his own initiative, more especially as his old enemy Montholon was a refugee in London, hatching plans with Prince Louis for the Boulogne *coup* which was to damp the spirits of the Bonapartists. Napoleon's chief heir had temporarily re-established his financial situation in 1826, with the help of a bequest: in spite of which he was still crippled by debts, and in danger of being arrested should be return to France, so naturally he was not included in the expedition.

Antommarchi was dead, as were the two abbés, Vignali and Buonavita, and the Irish Doctor O'Meara, but Louis Marchand who had tended the illustrious invalid 'like a friend', Saint-Denis, Pierron, Noverraz, Coursot and Archambault were to represent the imperial household – that handful of servants who had shared Napoleon's exile with filial abnegation.

There was some friction from the first, exactly as on the *Bellerophon* in 1815. Gourgaud wished to be treated on an equal footing with the Grand Marshal and looked down on poor Marchand, most unamiably, though he had been elevated from his rank of valet to executor of the will and was wearing the uniform of a lieutenant of the National Guard, which rank had been accorded him as the only means enabling him to sit at table with the Prince, an honour he coveted, or at least at that of the captain of *La Favorite*, which was to escort *La Belle-Poule*. Talleyrand's niece, the Duchesse de Dino, burst out laughing when she heard about this detail ... Honouring a valet! ... 'He will eat at the Prince's table. I abstain from comment.' During the voyage Gourgaud revived his old feud with Las Cases and then quarrelled with Hernoux, Joinville's aide-de-camp.

The coffin, in the shape of an ancient sarcophagus, had been ordered from a certain Le Marchand, a half-pay officer who had turned his hand to making furniture. It was a splendid affair, made of ebony polished till it looked like black marble, against which the letters NAPOLEON shone in copper gilt; handles and ornaments were in bronze gilt, as were the embossed Ns; the lock was concealed under a gold star. Victor Hugo was indignant that the letters were of copper: 'Copper gilt for Napoleon! Letters of gold! Letters of gold! That wouldn't be too much for him.' Inside was a lead lining, bearing the inscription, within a frame of laurels and arabesques:

Napoleon
Emperor and King
Died at St. Helena
May 5 1821

The pall was of purple velvet trimmed with ermine, with the corners set off by medallions decorated with the imperial eagle. On board *La Belle-Poule* a mortuary chapel had been erected, hung with black velvet sprinkled with gold stars and ornamented with silver tassels and candelabra. It was blessed by the bishop of Fréjus on June 22 along with all the crews entrusted with this holy mission. The cenotaph, supported by four eagles and surmounted by an imperial crown, was in Roman style, and the paintings in grisaille represented Justice, History, Religion, the Legion of Honour.

*   *   *

Joinville left Paris on July 2 and arrived at Toulon on July 6, where he and his officers, Captain Hernoux, his Chief of Staff and Lieutenant Touchard, his aide-de-camp, met with a warm welcome at a splendid dinner provided by the Port Admiral, Admiral Jurien de la Gravière. Next day, cheerful crowds – amongst whom there were perhaps – oh irony! – some survivors of the bloody anti-Bonapartist repressive measures of July 1815 – cheered the faithful of 1821. Bertrand, white-haired, in an old style lieutenant-general's uniform, and Marchand went on board the ships due to set sail that evening. Bertrand was already a legendary figure. It was known that he had been present at the Emperor's death, that he had scrupulously respected his sovereign's last wishes, and that this intransigent attitude had earned him the esteem of the royalist government; but that after having been Grand Marshal under the Empire he had refused to accept office at the court of Louis XVIII when his rank was restored to him. An old man, near his end and with precarious health, he had not hesitated to embark on this long voyage, reverently taking with him in his baggage his faded uniforms from those testing but glorious times, first giving to the King, to be placed on Napoleon's tomb, the sword of Austerlitz which Austria had refused to let him take to the Duke of Reichstadt. Along with Gourgaud, Emmanuel de Las Cases and four servants, he was Joinville's guest on *La Belle-Poule*, while Marchand and the Abbé Coquereau, chaplain to the expedition, were taken on board *La Favorite*.

How long that voyage of nearly three months must have seemed! Joinville listened amiably to the stories of the Emperor's companions in exile, and the ship's officers began reading the *Mémorial*. 'The conversation of those men who had witnessed so many events,' said the Prince later, 'and followed the Emperor in so many exploits, was particularly interesting. Every day we were subjected to a running fire of anecdotes and details, undoubtedly closer to the truth than many accounts written at leisure.' Gourgaud was inclined to sulk at times, because (just as in the evenings long ago at Longwood) he liked to be the centre of attention, but now he had occasionally to give way to Emmanuel de Las Cases or Bertrand, whose recollections were more fascinating than his fiery tirades. And the great man would shut himself in his cabin and note angrily 'This voyage is boring for everyone.'

After touching at Cadiz in mid-July, when the ships were on the high seas, Rohan-Chabot, in some distress, revealed the government's instructions to Joinville which Thiers had ordered him to keep secret until that moment, namely that he, a mere secretary to an embassy, was to be leader of the expedition. They had wished to avoid a conflict of authority between the King's son and the diplomat, two very young men and friends since childhood, but Joinville found this procedure wounding and had difficulty in putting a good face on his bad fortune.

By July 24 the ships had reached Madeira – where the inhabitants were still talking about the hurricane in 1815 when the *Northumberland* had passed by with Napoleon on board – and on the 27th they were at Teneriffe, for a stop of six days including the celebration of the anniversary of the July Revolution. On August 4 they crossed the tropic of Cancer, on their way to Brazil, where Joinville knew they would catch the north-west winds and be driven south to St. Helena. On the 20th it was the equator and on the 26th Bahia, where they stayed until September 14. After that came a long and monotonous voyage across the South Atlantic, where the ships were becalmed for six days, and Joinville was reduced to providing occupation for the crew in the form of exercises in fire-drill and clearing the decks for action. The Tropic of Capricorn was reached on the 20th, at longitude 35° West, and on the 23rd they had got to latitude 27° South. On October 6, after a period of calm, a fresh breeze got up from the south-east, strong enough to enable Joinville to announce to his passengers at noon on the 7th:

'Gentlemen, if as people say, St. Helena is visible from a long way off, we should soon be sighting it.'

At three o'clock the lookout in the yards announced that land was in sight: shrouded in dark clouds, the island was only fifty-five miles away.

The moment had arrived for the former exiles to relive their moving memories: twenty-five years ago, almost to the day, they had gazed upon the same scene while the Emperor examined the rock through his Austerlitz field-glasses . . .

*   *   *

During this period, while Paris was in a fever of excitement about the Emperor's return, it witnessed the unexpected sight of a Bonaparte appearing before the Chamber of Peers. Prince Louis, judging the climate favourable for a second *coup*, had disembarked on August 6 at Wimereux with a handful of supporters including Montholon, and planned to raise the garrison at Boulogne and march on the capital.

Since the end of 1838 he had been in London, living in style in his apartments in Carlton Gardens, driving around in a landau with the imperial arms on the doors, frequenting the Carlton, and entertained by the aristocracy. This tenaciously ambitious man, whom the French ambassador believed to be entirely absorbed in the wordly life of a dandy, had in fact been studiously keeping in touch with French affairs, carrying on a correspondence with his partisans, and even making a list of the persons who could back his cause and help his attempt when the moment came. He used sometimes to go to Portman Square to visit Mrs. Abell, a dark-haired young woman with a somewhat sad expression who talked to him about St. Helena, the Briars and the Emperor. Betsy Balcombe, for it was she, now a widow, was writing her *Recollections* and spoke freely about her memories of the past:

'His fascinating smile and kind manner removed every vestige of fear . . . (I did) a French translation every day and Napoleon would often condescend to look over them and correct my faults

... His smile and the expression of his eye could not be transmitted to canvas, and these constituted his chief charm.'*

The Prince was eager to hear everything about his uncle's gestures and attitudes, for he had not seen him since 1815 when he was only seven years old. One day he asked if his own curiously long, weak profile was like his uncle's?

'No!' declared Mrs. Abell laughing.

Well, it couldn't be helped, and the pretender came away from these interviews intoxicated by the thought of his tremendous heritage. A moment would come when the populace would remember, and then ...

To tell the truth the royalist government was expecting to see this obstinate trouble-maker appear on their frontiers. When Rémusat, the Home Secretary, warned the French ambassador in London in June: 'Bonapartism is very active,' he was rewarded by an alarming dispatch from Guizot: 'The party is strutting about and making a great noise ... They talk loudly and much; they describe their plans and their correspondence. They display their hopes ostentatiously. I know there is talk of equipping a vessel to attack the frigate returning from St. Helena with Napoleon's body on board, and carry it off as family property; or else to follow the French frigate and enter the port of Le Havre with it at all hazards.' None the less the shock was severe, and there was relief at Eu, where the King was resting, when they heard that a mere colonel of the Boulogne garrison had defeated the attempt.

What a strange sight! Louis Napoleon plunging into the sea to get back to his wretched boat amid shots fired by the Garde Nationale, while the King's son and two frigates were crossing the ocean to St. Helena to retrieve the mortal remains of the Emperor Napoleon ...

* Elizabeth, known as Betsy, Balcombe was the youngest daughter of the Balcombes, owners of the pavilion at The Briars, where Napoleon stayed from October 17 to December 10, 1815, when the work of enlarging Longwood House was finished.

The epilogue to this attempt could not have been more awkward for the government: on September 16, 1840, the Prince appeared before the upper house, elegant, completely assured, and opened his case straight away:

'I am here to represent before you a principle, a cause, a defeat. The principle is the sovereignty of the people; the cause that of the Empire; the defeat Waterloo. You have recognised the principle; you have served the cause; you wish to avenge the defeat.'

Most of the peers bore names that had been famous under the Empire, and they were struck by this calm audacity; such a one was President Pasquier, a baron by favour of Napoleon and former prefect of police, who now asked the ritual questions:*

'What is your profession?'

'French Prince in exile.'

'By what rights do you wear the Legion of Honour?'

'I found it in my cradle.'

However, the pretender did not make a great impression, with his medium height, his fair hair and moustaches, his Nordic, distant bearing; yet his voice was firm, and there were several who divined beneath his apparently expressionless mask that proud ambition and determination that belonged signally to the Bonapartes. The Advocate General defended the official case: 'The greatness of the Empire and the glory of the Emperor are not the patrimony of the family.' Nor were they the patrimony of the July Monarchy and those gathered together in its name; the royalist, Berryer, who was defending the Prince, furiously attacked all those peers who had been turncoats so often.†

---

* It was this same Pasquier who boasted of commanding a certain respect 'in spite of the thirteen oaths he had sworn'. Master of requests in the Council of State and prefect of police under Napoleon; Keeper of the Seals and Foreign Secretary under Louis XVIII, and President of the House of Peers and Chancellor of France under Louis Philippe, who made him a duke. He was a man who only had to go on living ...

† Pierre-Antoine Berryer (1790–1868). Although a legitimist he had helped his father defend Ney, and himself pleaded the cause of Cambronne, Lamennais and Chateaubriand.

The arrival of Napoleon's funeral cortège at the Invalides

The Catafalque in the Chapelle Ardente

'They want to turn you into judges, they want to make you deliver sentence on the Emperor's nephew. But who are you, after all? Counts, barons, those of you who were ministers, generals, senators or marshals, to whom do you owe your titles, your distinctions?'

A cruel reminder, and a cruel reply of the Prince's when he was summoned to reveal the names of his accomplices:

'Everyone in this assembly, if I had succeeded . . .'

The infuriated peers thought it safest to imprison for life this dangerous and audacious recidivist, who was so good at having the last word: he got into the vehicle which was to take him to the fortress of Ham, and noticing a gendarme in an ill-fitting uniform, remarked laconically to the officer escorting him:

'When I'm in power I'll see to all that.'*

* Montholon had been condemned to twenty years imprisonment in the same fortress: he only served six, for he was pardoned in July 1846 after the Prince's escape, this merciful gesture being inspired by Gourgaud, then in favour. Montholon showed his gratitude in his *Récits de la Captivité*, where he tried – a difficult task – to justify the conduct at Longwood of the man with whom he had come close to fighting a duel under Napoleon's eyes.

VII

'LA BELLE-POULE' AT ST. HELENA

✳

The population of St. Helena was not favourably disposed towards the removal of Napoleon's body, which ever since 1821 had brought fame, and therefore some material profit to the island.

First there had been Torbett, the owner of the land in which the grave had been dug; after pocketing an indemnity of £650 and an annual rent of £50 'for the damage caused to his estate', he had in 1826 got the East India Company to pay him a capital sum of £1,200 for giving free access to visitors. Some years later Torbett found himself short of cash and mortgaged his land, so that after his death his creditors became the owners, his widow having been unable to pay off a debt of £2,700. But everyone, headed by the local administration, got some profit from it: ships of every nation anchored in Jamestown bay, and their passengers, amazed by the sinister appearance of the rock – like a dungeon sprung from the waves fully armed – crowded into local boats, the only ones able to brave the rollers, which broke, sometimes for weeks on end on the landing-stage, and made their way along the clay track called Side Path, to the solitary tomb in Sane Valley.

It seemed very silent there, after so much noise elsewhere. It might have been the last abode of a disillusioned philosopher, the Ermenonville of some island Rousseau. All round the wide paving-stones surrounded by cast-iron railings formerly intended to enclose the prisoner, stretched the romantic landscape made famous by engravings – willows, partly stripped of their leaves by souvenir-hunters, lent a pleasant shade, and close by, the spring flowed between gigantic cannas, begonias and geraniums. The

owners of the place turned everything to account, selling food to
tired travellers, washed down with a glass of spring water, now as
precious as Jordan water, and so made a comfortable income . . .
Travellers, much refreshed, wrote their names in a register in the
cabin of the English guardian, an elderly disabled man employed
to look after the place, and then returned by the rough path along
which the heavy coffin of the god of battles had been carried one
day in May 1821. They climbed into their carriages again and
drove to Longwood, now converted into a farm by the East
India Company. At Hutt's Gate they were shown the Grand
Marshal's house, where a Mrs. Dickson, former servant to the
Comtesse Bertrand, sold strong liquor; then they wandered in the
deserted gardens of the last imperial palace . . . A gloomy sight . . .
Inside the house they were stupefied to find a granary full of corn
in the drawing-room where the most famous prisoner in history
had expired, and stables in what had been his bedroom. On June
5, 1823, the Colonial government, presided over by Brigadier-
General Walker, had decided to convert the buildings at Longwood into a farm, on the curious pretext 'that no more useful and
necessary function could be provided for them'. The excursion
was distressing and poignant. Or so it seemed to some sailors who
had no scruples about adding honest comments after their signatures, but no one was likely to complain, since at the end of the
outing their money was transferred into the drivers' pockets and
helped preserve a semblance of prosperity.

After the body was removed, what would become of guides,
horses and bars? That was the first, sordidly material question to
be asked when the brig *Dolphin*, having left England on May 21,
arrived on July 8 with the unexpected news that 'the mortal remains
of the Emperor Napoleon were to be removed to France'. A local
official who wrote a good hand and had literary leanings, incor-
porated a phrase of Byron's in one of his reports:

'But France shall feel the want of this last consolation.'

But the naïve population who, according to the same scribe,
had believed they were to be able to exploit this gold-mine 'until

the trumpets sound for the Last Judgement', lamented the loss of their earnings and tried to console themselves by dreaming of the fine festivities which would accompany so great an event.

In great haste His Excellency the governor, Major-General Middlemore, gave orders to Captain Alexander, commanding the Engineers, to construct a hearse and make arrangements for opening 'the Emperor's' tomb, and also to prepare a mahogany coffin in case the one dating from 1821 should have suffered any damage. So there was no more talk of 'General Bonaparte', and 'Bony'. Nothing was sumptuous enough, according to local opinion, for 'the late Emperor Napoleon'.

As the *Dolphin* had spotted a French frigate near the equator, the inhabitants took their walks in the direction of Jamestown quay, so as to be sure not to miss the arrival of this magnificent vessel, said to carry sixty guns. Captain Alexander worked at double speed, and with the aid of a rickety calash belonging to a former governor created, as in a fairy tale, a magnificent chariot, swallowed up in black draperies: for lack of enough lengths of velvet he had however to fall back on satin, which was also used as a border to the pall, made of some more ordinary stuff.

Days passed, then weeks. Sometimes the promenaders would stop and stare at the grey smear of some large ship on the horizon. First, in August, it was the *Buckinghamshire* and the *Repulse*, two small ships belonging to the East India Company, which attracted no interest. On the 21st someone shouted 'the frigate!' and the port officials put on their smartest uniforms and hurried to greet the arrival, which turned out to be merely *La Coraline*, on its way from Pondicherry and Réunion, with the Marquis de Saint-Simon (former governor of the French Indies) on board. On September 7 Dumont d'Urville's famous *Astrolabe* was seen to drop anchor, along with Captain Jacquinot's *Zélée*, returning from a voyage of exploration in the Antarctic; then on the 14th the *Junon*, a transport ship from Réunion. Dumont d'Urville had left Toulon in September 1837 to explore the Antarctic and reconnoitre some of the South Sea Islands. He reached latitude 65° South, took possession of Adelie Land and was due back at Toulon in November 1840. Even the most optimistic were becoming discouraged when on October 7 the brig *Oreste* commanded by Lieutenant-Commander Doret came to revive their hopes.* This ship had left France on July 31, accompanied by *La Gloire* and *La Boussole* under the orders of Admiral Mackau, to reinforce the blockade of Buenos Aires, but at Dakar they had been diverted to take dispatches to the Prince de Joinville at St. Helena, and her Captain supposed *La Belle-Poule* and *La Favorite* to be already on their way back to France, their mission accomplished . . .

Next morning the semaphore on Prosperous Bay signalled the approach of two ships, a frigate and a corvette: the wind was slight and blowing first from the south and then from the east, forcing the ships to fetch about and have some difficulty in reaching Jamestown in the teeth of wild gusts off the land. On the bridge stood officers and crew, silent with emotion, grouped round the Emperor's former companions and observing every detail of the barren landscape, the jagged rocks plunging vertically into the foaming sea, the strangely coloured beds of lava, the bare countryside broken here and there by a few huts, the trees twisted by the wind. They were shown George Island, a bastion swallowed up by the angry surge of the sea and given over to seabirds alone, and the Barn, a sombre sentinel of tormented rock, whose profile against the sky was reminiscent of the Emperor's own. According to some, it was on this island that the gypsum was found in 1821 from which the plaster for Napoleon's death-mask was made. It is more probable that the mineral was collected in Prosperous Bay Plain, closer to Longwood, the approach to George Island being somewhat dangerous. As they passed

---

* Doret had been among the young officers involved in the plot to help Napoleon escape to the United States in July 1815, by leaving the roadstead of the Ile d'Aix on two *chasse-marées* of twelve tons. Deprived of his rank by Louis XVIII; it was restored to him by Louis Philippe in 1830.

beneath the semaphore at Prosperous Bay someone pointed out the gay note of colour made by the foliage of the gum-trees at Longwood; within that little plantation the exiles had often tried to keep boredom at bay by walking in a circle like convicts.

At three o'clock *La Belle-Poule* dropped anchor in Jamestown Bay, followed by *La Favorite* at six o'clock. It was very like the picture sketched for them by Las Cases: a few ramparts, guns in every hole in the rocks, a poor-looking church, some small houses covered in faded paint, and the Castle (government head-quarters) flying the Union Jack. Already boats were speeding over the sea filled with men in uniform, who ranged themselves along the shore while the other frigate was still under way. Captain Hernoux received Captain Middlemore (the governor's son), Captain Alexander, Captain Barnes of the garrison, Saul Solomon (the French consul), William Janisch (former secretary to Hudson Lowe and now employed by the East India Company), and some officers from the *Dolphin*, Lieutenants Littlehale and Rowe. While Joinville supervised the ship's manoeuvres these visitors passed the time chatting to Generals Bertrand and Gourgaud, and visited the mortuary chapel on board, which left them speechless. Louis Philippe's son, a tall figure, with his aristocratic face partly concealed by a carefully trimmed sailor's beard and his serious yet confident tone, made an excellent impression, and all St. Helena agreed that this Frenchman was a 'real gentleman'. When Captain Alexander offered him the rooms in the Castle formerly refused to Napoleon, he declined charmingly, saying:

'My ship is my house.'

The governor had put himself to some expense. He had made ready several rooms in the Castle for the Prince, with a dinner-table for thirty. He had also rented the chief house in the town for the members of his suite, as well as the best carriages and horses.

As if to efface the memory of the unfortunate humiliations of 1815, a spectacular, carefully organised ceremony enlivened the little port: as the *Oreste* docked, her crew greeted Joinville with shouts of 'Long live the King!' from the yards, after which the *Dolphin* favoured him with a salute of twenty-one guns. *La Belle-Poule* slowly hoisted the Union Jack and replied with a royal salute, which was at once answered by the fort on Ladder Hill and the *Dolphin*: the din was terrific and the echoes rolled up the valley, terrifying thousands of birds and sending them streaking the sky with shrill cries.

Joinville having decided to visit the governor next morning, young Las Cases was the first to mix with the crowds of onlookers on the quay, in search of memories of his childhood. The sad little town was swarming with sailors, women dressed in their best and natives in rags. 'I contemplated everything around me slowly, hardly able to believe my eyes, experiencing what one feels when waking from a dream . . . My memories were as alive and real as if our captivity had only ceased the day before.' There it was that twenty-three years ago, a sickly, nervous adolescent, he had suffered the unforgettable humiliation of embarking with his father under the malicious eyes of Lowe's myrmidons, after being snatched away from Napoleon's suite by an infamous subterfuge. He had grown, he had become a man and an official personage, but the images left by those extraordinary years were imprinted on his memory for ever. He stopped before the Castle, moist-eyed; it was there he had spent the last days of exile, and that his father had said goodbye to Bertrand and Gourgaud. He recognised Solomon's shop, where the ladies of Longwood used to buy stuffs and trinkets. He looked about for the tavern where Cipriani, the Emperor's major-domo, who was a talented collector of information, used to hang about and drink with sailors so as to gather news of the free world for his master. Next morning he met Lieutenant-Colonel Hodson and Andrew Darling.*
While Napoleon and Las Cases were camping at The Briars, they

---

* Lieutenant-Colonel Hodson (a major at the time) (1779–1858) belonged to the St. Helena regiment in 1815. Napoleon liked him and invited him to Longwood.

Darling kept a personal museum, and sold certain coveted relics to the French: the Emperor's bath, a sofa, the Longwood aviary, a table and a *pied de roi*.

had escaped to the house of the former one evening when Admiral Cockburn was giving a ball at the Castle: Hodson remembered proudly that the great man had nicknamed him Hercules, because he was so tall. Darling had been given the unwelcome task – but that applied to all tasks under Hudson Lowe's rod of iron – of maintaining the furniture of Longwood House in good condition, and attending to the needs of the exiles, and his last mission had been to make the coffins in 1821. But this was a time for goodwill and politeness, and the three men met with loud expressions of pleasure, like old friends.

Next day, October 9, a Friday, Joinville paid a return visit to the Captain of the *Dolphin*, and was greeted by a salute of twenty-one guns, to which *La Belle-Poule* replied; then, accompanied by Rohan-Chabot, Bertrand, Gourgaud and his aide-de-camp, he went ashore in full uniform to visit the governor, who was ill and awaiting him at Plantation House. Another salvo from the *Dolphin*, returned by *La Belle-Poule*, then Lieutenant-Colonel Trelawney, the oldest officer of the garrison, bowed to the Prince on the quay, and introduced the guard of honour, a hundred men of the 91st regiment. At the Castle an hour's halt was made, and all the important civilians and soldiers bowed to the son of the French King in the large room which had once been Sir Hudson Lowe's office.

The French did not stop long at Plantation House, as they were in a hurry to visit the Tomb in the company of Captain Alexander, the Colonial Judge (W. Wilde) and two British officers.

'Gentlemen, on Thursday 15th Napoleon's mortal remains will be handed over to you,' the governor confirmed at the close of the interview.

The road winding down to Sane Valley and Longwood was haunted by phantoms of the Emperor's exile: closing their eyes, his companions once again saw Hudson Lowe, draped in his long cloak, hurrying along in drenching rain to interrogate the Grand Marshal as if he were a corporal, or discussing with

Montholon the allocation of rations, or tackling 'Bonaparte' about some money matter. Perhaps Bertrand and Marchand were remembering the Emperor's last outing in October 1820: hunched on his saddle, his face pale and his features drawn, Napoleon had gone as far as the shining semi-circle of Sandy Bay, ceaselessly battered by the ocean, while his pitiless guardian squatted on a hill following his movements through field-glasses. In twenty-five years the scene had changed; thanks to the works on the water supply ordered by Lowe, Longwood now possessed several meagre pastures, and the trees now growing on the higher ground softened the chaotic decor of former days. In this month of October the rainy season was just over, and plants were springing up, while the brilliant colours of tropical species were an agreeable surprise to those who had been fed on Las Cases' gloomy descriptions.

Bertrand, Gourgaud and Marchand trembled as they entered the rocky path leading to the bottom of the valley: they were reliving every moment of that May day in 1821, when they had followed that simple coffin under the frosty gaze of their guardians. There was the same silence now, only broken by the wind rustling in the trees or the cheerful whistle of a canary; the same sweetish smell of cedarwood, suggestive of incense, the same cryptlike coolness. Suddenly they recognised, submerged in the shadow of the willows near the sentry box in which a soldier stood guard, the black wooden gate and the nameless tombstone ... The Abbé Coquereau was already on his knees, praying. Joinville, very pale, removed his hat and slowly walked round the railing, stooping to pick a flower. The border of flowers surrounding the tomb was beautifully kept: Marchand, who had fallen on his knees on those stones before he left the island in 1821, recognised the plants flowering so gaily in this haven of shade and freshness. One of the willows had died, and the other had been stripped of its leaves by visitors and was bent with age. The spring vanished into a carpet of cannas, moon lilies and arums.

One of the pensioners employed to care for the tomb, Mrs. Torbett (widow of the owner of the valley), and a friend of hers, Mrs. Loudon who owned a cottage near by, were covertly following every move made by the French, and Joinville at once gave orders for each to be given a handful of gold and the promise of a pension for life to compensate them for the loss they would suffer; the two guardians, John King and John Young, also received gratuities from the French government. Then he ordered the dead willow to be carried away on a hand-cart, sawed up and the pieces distributed to the members of the expedition, after which he set off for Longwood.

He found a scene of desolation. The farmer who had leased the house from the East India Company, had installed within it hugger-mugger, stables, piggery, granary and farmyard. As a last straw it was raining, and Marchand had difficulty in dissipating the melancholy visible on all their faces, by explaining that in the Emperor's time the house, 'small though it was, was well-cared-for and surrounded by greenery and pretty gardens which gave it a certain charm'. There was nothing to recall the past except a deal table, a register full of signatures, and some clumsy inscriptions: 'After having been a grenadier in the Garde, Michel Robert signed on as a sailor on the *Amélie*, and went to salute the home of his little corporal. Adieu.' And again: 'I was devilish fond of you when you were alive, I like you much more now you are dead. Courtois of the 27th.' Close to the door: 'Alive, the world; dead, six feet of earth,' and 'Such a death was needed after such a life. The work of Providence is complete.'

Joinville went bareheaded into the first room, the one that had served as antechamber and billiard-room; the humidity had made the walls leprous: not a stick of furniture, merely the mark where a mirror had hung over the remains of a chimney-piece. In the next room, where Napoleon had died, a threshing-machine was stored: the floor was rotten, the torn wall-paper revealed stone and clay, windows and doors were broken, graffiti and dates covered every fragment of woodwork left intact. Feeling embarrassed, the

English members of the party vanished discreetly, while the shattered Marchand poured out his recollections:

'He lay there.'

'With his head turned this way,' specified Bertrand.

They were all picturing the Emperor, in the watches of the night, his elbow resting on the arm of his chair, turning the pages of the book of his legend in that room where soon his death-rattle would be heard. Albine de Montholon would be drowsing on a sofa while the talk of wars, conquests, treaties and reforms went on.

'You are asleep, Madame . . . What time is it? Let's go to bed.'

One day he had gone to bed there never to get up again.

The dining-room and the library were now being used as a shed, and were cluttered with farm implements. The Emperor's private rooms, his closet and bedroom, had had the partitions removed and were doing duty as stables: the ground was covered with manure and a manger stood in place of the table where he had scribbled notes for dictation. Arthur Bertrand clenched his fists with rage. 'Everything that existed in the Emperor's day has so completely vanished that it's impossible not to think it must have been done on purpose; but if they wanted to destroy these mute but eloquent witnesses of his savage treatment they should not have stopped at soiling these walls, they should have pulled them down.'

The gardens, once laid out with difficulty in the un-productive soil and lovingly tended by the servants, had disappeared too: no sunken alleys, no grotto, no Chinese pavilion, no arbour, but the everlastings sown in 1819 had spread all round the house and on the plateau, and their golden and green buds were on the point of bursting. The big ornamental pond in the shape of a half-moon was still there, being used as a drinking-trough, and one or two trees; Las Cases recognised one of them at the corner of an avenue . . . It was the one Napoleon was sitting on, on the day when Lowe came to arrest the author of the *Mémorial* with his own hand. The pavilions occupied by the Montholons, the

Las Cases, Gourgaud, the priests and the doctor, had been turned into stables, a hen-house and a pigsty.

It was still raining when the French started back to Jamestown. At Hutt's Gate they found waiting for them the same Miss Mason who had so often amused them by riding to meet them on a docile bullock, and the widow Dickson who had been Arthur Bertrand's nurse. Their meeting was like a ray of sunlight. Gourgaud smiled and Arthur Bertrand shed a few tears. At The Briars they saw the pavilion from the road (it was now occupied by Colonel Trelawney) buried in its bushy gardens, the trellised arbour where Napoleon used to work, and the philosophers' alley where he paced with Las Cases at dusk.

During dinner at the Castle that evening, presided over by Colonel Trelawney in the governor's name, they were all lost in their memories. The band of *La Belle-Poule* played soft music, and the beau monde of the island forgot the past and enjoyed this elegant entertainment. Joinville returned to his ship late that night, while some of the officers preferred to put up at Solomon's, where bed and board were provided, exactly as in 1815.*

Next day the Prince dined at Plantation House, with Rohan-Chabot, Bertrand, Gourgaud and Las Cases, received guests on *La Belle-Poule* and honoured the officers' mess at Jamestown with his presence, nor did he escape the obligations of these crushing colonial formalities until the afternoon of Thursday the 13th when he went off, to make a drawing of the tomb and pay another visit to Longwood.† The ships' crews made the same pilgrimage, and returned with their arms full of souvenirs, plants, flowers, fragments of woodwork and bags of earth. The Emperor's ex-companions visited various familiar places: Maldivia, still occupied by the Hodsons, and Mount Pleasant by old Sir William

* This was a last chance to make some money, and we have before us the bill for the hospitality provided: £609 for seven days including baths at 7s 6d each and refreshments during the exhumation at £1 5s . . .

† The Prince was a very good draughtsman; his sketches of St. Helena are in the collection of the Comte de Paris. Henri Durand-Brayer, the marine painter, a passenger on the *Oreste*, has also left interesting pictures of these events.

Doveton, who was quite amazed by all the excitement over the exhumation of a man whom he had treated informally, not even removing his hat, in order to please Lowe ... Marchand asked after Esther Vesey, the daughter of an English sergeant whom he would have married in 1817, had not the Emperor objected: she was dead, and the son she had borne him, James Octave, had been deported to the Cape for bad behaviour.

*   *   *

On the eve of the day fixed for the exhumation a detachment of the 91st regiment, commanded by Lieutenant Barney, set out in the afternoon ahead of the hearse, the springs of which had been hastily strengthened so that they should not give way under the weight of the sarcophagus brought from France. Rohan-Chabot's reports lead one to think that there was some friction between French and British authorities over the formalities of the exhumation. 'From the first day the Prince de Joinville suggested to the governor that his crews should undertake the work of exhumation and the removal, which His Royal Highness would in that case supervise in person; but General Middlemore had received formal orders from his government to be responsible himself for all the operations until the imperial coffin arrived at the place of embarkation, and had therefore to decline the Prince's offer.' Middlemore was an old soldier and an awkward character. The first governor appointed by the government after the island was taken over by the East India Company, he had taken possession of his post with a brusqueness reminiscent of an occupying army, and his arbitrary methods antagonised even the inhabitants – who criticised his intransigent attitude towards the French.*

After the dinner given by Joinville on board the frigate, all those who were to be present at the ceremony set off in their turn

---

* He was replaced in 1842 by Colonel Trelawney, who gained nothing but praise from the French expedition and was well received by the population.

along the road to the valley. The French were represented by Rohan-Chabot, Bertrand and his son, Emmanuel de Las Cases, Gourgaud, Marchand, the Abbé Coquereau and two choir-boys, Captain Guyet of *La Favorite*, Captain Doret of *L'Oreste*: Captain Charner and Dr. Guillard from *La Belle-Poule*, Saint-Denis, Pierron, Archambault, Noverraz and a lead-worker. Joinville remained on board, offended because his crews were not allowed to undertake the operation. The English had chosen Captain Alexander to act as commissioner, and also present were Judge Wilde, Colonel Trelawney, Colonel Hodson, William Seale (secretary to the government), Captain Littlehale of the *Dolphin*, and Andrew Darling who had arranged the funeral in 1821, as well as two foremen from the service of public works and the engineers.

An icy wind was blowing and the rain was falling in torrents in the sinister Devil's Punchbowl; the British soldiers, whose job it was to keep inquisitive people at bay, had set up two tents close to the tombstone, one as a shelter the other as a chapel. Shadowy figures came and went in an agonising silence, workmen armed with picks and shovels and soldiers in red uniforms carrying lanterns, while the moon occasionally emerged from her canopy of clouds and threw an unreal light on the conqueror's last bivouac, revealing soaked tunics and faces hollow-eyed from fatigue and emotion.

First of all the geraniums and bulbous plants growing round the tombstone were pulled up (Joinville had asked to have them to distribute to his sailors), next the workmen threw down the heavy metal grille, raised the three flagstones and began to clear away the thick layer of clay filling the top part of the grave. Not until three o'clock in the morning, and at a depth of two metres, did the sappers' picks at last reach the layer of Roman cement, twenty-five centimetres deep, which closed the vault and adhered firmly to the walls. Chisels and hammers came into use, while Captain Alexander, despairing of finishing the work in time for the funeral procession to take place during the day, decided to have a trench dug on the left of the grave, so as to reach the coffin should the cement resist the workmen's efforts. The soldiers worked their hardest and towards eight o'clock the last fragments of masonry finally gave way: revealing a flagstone which they set about raising with the help of a derrick. Between the bed of cement and the stone coffin there was a layer of mortar twenty-seven centimetres thick, made of rubble and iron tenons. It was daylight by now, but the rain went on falling without respite and the officers went into the tent to put on their uniforms. At half-past nine the mahogany coffin came into view, as well as the straps by which it had been lowered. The Abbé Coquereau began to chant the *De Profundis*; then the two commissioners, Rohan-Chabot and Alexander, went down into the grave to examine the coffin, one corner of which seemed to have suffered from the damp. This quadruple coffin rested on flagstones, which were themselves supported by rubble, but the spring flowed only a few metres away producing constant humidity.

As soon as they had climbed out again, Dr. Guillard instructed that holes be pierced at both head and feet of the coffin, which was then lifted out of its stone niche and laid to the left of the grave, before being carried by twelve bare-headed soldiers into the tent where the Abbé Coquereau recited the Commendatory prayers. English law insisted that the opening of a coffin observed certain preliminary formalities and Judge Wilde raised some objections. Rohan-Chabot and Alexander protested that they had the governor's permission, but 'His Honour' obstinately insisted that his remarks should figure in the report. The screws had to be sawn through to open the first mahogany covering, which was warped on the outside, and to remove the leaden coffin; this was at once placed in the sarcophagus brought from France, at the very moment when the governor arrived, having been kept informed of the progress of events, followed by Joinville's aide-de-camp, Lieutenant Touchard. The lead cracked under the chisel, the screw in the second mahogany coffin turned easily and the tinplate of the last envelope was cut along the line of its original

welding.* They gathered shoulder to shoulder, but could at first
only make out what looked like a recumbent effigy, outlined by
the satin covering loosened by the passage of the years. The
sound of breathing was louder than that of the spring when Dr.
Guillard slowly rolled back this material, from feet to head, and
at last exposed the Emperor's corpse to view. Faces marked by the
strain and exhaustion of this icy wake suddenly froze. They were
expecting to find formless remains, only identifiable by some
shreds of uniform, but here was Napoleon, covered in a sort of
greyish mould but perfectly recognisable, and apparently peacefully sleeping. Bertrand and Marchand, who had stayed to the end,
recognised through their tears the slight rictus of the death-agony
which had uncovered three very white teeth; the head they had
laid on a white satin cushion seemed enormous; there were still a
few eye-lashes on the lids, the thin lips half-opened, the chin
bluish with a slight beard, and the beautiful hands seemed alive,
particularly the left which Bertrand had kissed before the burial
and then placed on the thigh. The finger-nails had grown after
death and were pale as marble, as were four toe-nails visible
through one boot that had given at the seams. Although the wings
of the nose had fallen in a little, the cheeks were swollen and the
eyeballs sunk in their orbits, Marchand commented that the
corpse was more like the Emperor than the dead man of 1821. As
Gourgaud said later: 'One must have loved the Emperor as I did
to understand what was going on in my soul when Dr. Guillard
permitted us to see, through floods of tears, the mortal remains of
our hero.'

The doctor felt the eyelids and found them hardened, the
hands, 'firm like those of a mummy', the limbs having kept their
shape although shrunken in size, the thorax and the stomach
strongly depressed, sunken from having the entrails removed,
and remarked in amazement that the skin retained a colour
'usually only seen in life'.

* The first mahogany coffin was sawn up and distributed among the French
crews: every reliquary of St. Helena contains a fragment.

The clothes were barely soiled. Under the famous uniform of the light cavalry of the Imperial Guard could be seen the ribbon of the Legion of Honour and the white waistcoat. The hat lay on the legs, partly hiding the kerseymere breeches. The gold braid, epaulettes, stars and decorations were blackened, but the gold crown of the *croix des braves* still glittered softly. When Guillard wiped away the mould covering the boots with the back of his hand the leather appeared to be intact. Bertrand and Marchand recognised all the silver objects they had placed in the coffin at the time of burial, including two vases containing the heart and stomach placed between the legs; these had assumed a dusky bronze colour and adhered so firmly to the body that the doctor dared not remove them to examine them. It was as if time had stood still for twenty years; Bertrand, with his white hair and face lined by age, and Marchand then a handsome dark-haired young man and now a portly fifty-year-old, were silent with emotion and with their eyes full of tears, thinking they must be dreaming awake.

After the body had been exposed to the air for about two minutes, Rohan-Chabot gave orders for the coffins to be rapidly re-sealed. Guillard covered the corpse with the quilted satin and sprinkled it with creosote, then the workmen completed their task and the Emperor disappeared for ever from the eyes of the living. The three envelopes of 1821, tinplate, mahogany and lead, were screwed inside those of the sarcophagus: Napoleon now lay in a sextuple coffin, proof against time and weather, and Alexander handed the gilt key to the French commissioner. According to Emmanuel de Las Cases, the tinplate lining was not re-soldered as it was badly rusted. Beside the three coffins of 1821, there was a leaden envelope (separated from the original bier by sawdust and wooden corners) one of ebony and one of oak, to protect the gilding on the sarcophagus.

It was one o'clock and the Englishman closed the ceremony by reading a short announcement: the witnesses having been assured of the presence of the Emperor Napoleon's body in the coffin, he had orders to direct the funeral procession to proceed to Jamestown where His Excellency the governor would officially deliver the mortal remains to the Prince de Joinville. Rohan-Chabot was expressing his thanks, when a bareheaded English officer in full uniform was seen running towards them through the rain, followed by two aides-de-camp: it was Major-General Churchill, chief of staff of the Indian army, who had arrived from Bombay the evening before and was bringing the homage of Marlborough's family to the greatest captain in history.

Forty-three soldiers, making a supreme effort, managed to carry the enormous coffin, which now weighed 1,200 kilos, as far as the hearse waiting on the track from the tomb to the Jamestown road. There twenty or so of them were needed to help the horses pull the wheels out of the wet clay. The French had covered the hearse with the imperial cloak brought from Paris, a gorgeous pall that looked all the more amazing in these rustic surroundings: it was of purple velvet, embroidered with gold bees, bordered with ermine, and with an N at each corner, crowned and embossed with a silver cross. Bertrand, Marchand, Gourgaud and Emmanuel de Las Cases carried the tassels.

A little before half-past three the cannon at Alarm House was fired to announce the departure of the convoy, then the fort on High Knoll and the *Dolphin* followed suit, and fired at intervals of a minute until the arrival at Jamestown. On reaching the road the procession formed behind the detachment of artillery of the St. Helena Militia, entrusted with the task of clearing the way by driving off curious spectators, donkeys and cattle. In front came three companies of the 91st regiment, commanded by Captain Blackwell, next the Militia, 220 men strong with its band and commanded by Lieutenant-Colonel Seale. The Abbé Coquereau, preceded by two choir-boys one carrying the cross and the other the censer, walked praying several paces in front of the hearse, as it was dragged and then held back with difficulty on the steep road down to the town by four horses caparisoned in black, their bridles held by grooms in mourning and escorted by soldiers of the Royal Artillery. Marchand and Gourgaud carried the gold tassels on the left, Bertrand and Emmanuel de Las Cases those on the right. Pierron, Saint-Denis, Archambault and Novarrez walked behind, wearing mourning for the second time for the master whose service had given them a place on the fringes of history. The Comte de Rohan-Chabot, chief mourner, walked behind the little group of the faithful, surrounded by Captains Charner (second officer of *La Belle-Poule*) and Guyet of *La Favorite*, Arthur Bertrand, Coursot, Captain Doret and Dr. Guillard. The officers of the garrison and other notables, all in mourning and walking in step, were followed by General Middle-more who braved his illness to walk six kilometres, supported by the Judge and Colonel Hodson. General Churchill and Major Johnson, passengers on *La Belle-Alliance*, kept a little ahead of the inhabitants and a detachment of the Royal Artillery which brought up the rear of the procession.

There was a certain majesty in this splendid military display on a miserable rock in the middle of the ocean. Now the British guns and those of *La Belle-Poule* were thundering in unison in honour of the man who had so often unloosed the storms of battle with a wave of his hand. Some of the artillerymen had been under fire at Waterloo, and they made a respectful escort to the man who was one of them before he became Emperor. With them were two generals in red uniforms, one of whom descended from the victor of Malplaquet. The emotion of Napoleon's companions in exile, as they brought to life their memories of 1821, the youthful enthusiasm of the French crews for whom the expedition to St. Helena was a splendid adventure in an ordinary sailor's life, all this was what would have been desired by this sovereign born of the people, whose true greatness was expressed in theatrical simplicity, and whose grey overcoat eclipsed his marshals' uniforms. Perhaps he would also have decided that the two hours' calvary of the old governor-general redeemed the meanness and ferocity of Sir Hudson Lowe, who had lived long enough to hear from his cottage on the shores of the Thames the echo of the guns of St.

Helena as they saluted the body of the exile he had converted into a martyr.

The paths overlooking Jamestown were lined with groups of spectators, who ran over the pebbles, anxious not to miss a minute of the display, as soon as the sound of the funeral march announced that the procession was approaching. It was five o'clock, and the leading detachment was marching in two lines, one on each side of the single road, with arms reversed. British flags were at half-mast, including those of the consulates, shops were shut, and every window was crowded with onlookers. *La Belle-Poule*, *La Favorite* and *l'Oreste* as well as the French merchant ships, *La Bonne-Aimée* (Captain Gallet) and *L'Indien* (Captain Truquetil) displayed royal mourning, with yards apeak.

When the hearse had passed through the postern and come out on to the sea front, the 91st regiment was still marching with arms reversed, amid the uproar of artillery. A few steps from the quay Joinville stood awaiting them, the red ribbon of the Empire crossing his chest, and surrounded by his staff officers all in deep mourning. Half-dead with exhaustion, General Middlemore advanced with short steps and announced that he was handing over the body in the name of his government. It was the end of the most horrible misunderstanding in history. Joinville thanked him with obvious emotion in the name of France for the signs of sympathy and respect which had accompanied the ceremony. A launch moored to the quay was smothered under the folds of a huge tricolour flag: the coffin was lowered into it while the band of *La Belle-Poule* struck up funeral music. At the exact moment symbolising the end of the Emperor's exile, the batteries on shore boomed forth once more, to be answered by those of the ships, as they straightened their yards and decked themselves with flags. From the mast of the launch floated a silk flag, embroidered with a regal N by the ladies of the island ... so much noise, such complaisance, such attentions, after so long a silence and such contempt!

Joinville took the tiller, Captain Guyet stationed himself in the bows, while the Abbé Coquereau, Bertrand, Marchand, Gourgaud and Emmanuel de Las Cases stood around the sarcophagus in the same places they had occupied in the procession; then the twenty rowers leant on their oars and nothing was heard except the sound of the blades striking the water slowly and solemnly and the hushed music playing on the quay. Suddenly the batteries on shore began firing again, followed by those on the ships, in honour of the outlaw returning to his homeland. The wonder-struck crowds tried to imprint these last images on their memory: the dinghies of *La Favorite* were lighting the way and those of *La Belle-Poule* acted as escorts on either side of the large launch loaded almost to sinking-point, while those of the *Oreste* made up the rear, their sailors bareheaded and with crêpe bands on their arms. A second salute from the French rent the air, then a third, leaving a cloud of gunpowder reddening in the rays of the setting sun.

The sailors of *La Belle-Poule* stood motionless on the yards, drums rolling, hats in hand, and a guard of honour of sixty men commanded by the oldest lieutenant, Penanros, stood with arms reversed while the coffin passed between two ranks of officers, borne now by Frenchmen. Although it was dark, the Abbé Coquereau read the prayers of intercession for the dead by the light of lanterns hanging from the fo'c'sle which had been arranged as a chapel and decorated with flags and fasces, then, dropping with exhaustion, he prepared to watch beside the corpse till dawn: with four sentries and an officer. *La Belle-Poule* had kept all her flags flying, and the mourning flag embroidered at St. Helena floated from the mainmast: silence fell at last and the tropical night spread its baldachin sown with stars over the hero's mortal remains.

*   *   *

Next day, a Friday, a funeral mass was held on *La Belle-Poule*, and at eight o'clock *La Favorite* and *L'Oreste* set their yards apeak. The Emperor's companions took their places round the bier, while Lieutenant Penanros arranged his guard of honour on each side. At the foot were Joinville, Rohan-Chabot, the ships' captains and staff officers, Solomon the French consul, and all the sailors of the division. The cannon fired a salute at the moment when Coquereau was intoning the mass for the dead, and *La Favorite* and *L'Oreste* fired minute-guns. At the elevation of the host the drum rolled and thousands of men fell on their knees. All those present, beginning with Louis Philippe's son, joined in the prayers for the dead, and then the coffin was taken down into the mortuary chapel between decks, where it was to remain until their arrival in France.

Joinville wanted to set sail at once, but Rohan-Chabot and commissioner Chèdeville of *La Belle-Poule* still had to draw up the official report with Captain Alexander, a proceeding which lasted all day long on the 17th and part of the night.* All this trouble deserved payment, and Alexander was presented with a gold snuff-box set with diamonds and a portrait of Louis Philippe, Colonel Trelawney received a richly inlaid sporting rifle, the workmen who had carried out the exhumation £200, and the poor of the island £300. Miss Gideon, who had organised the embroidery of the satin flag, nearly fainted with joy on receiving a beautifully engraved bracelet. All those who had taken part in the ceremonies were given a silver or bronze medal, one side bearing the inscription: 'Law of June 10, 1840, directing that the mortal remains of the Emperor Napoleon be moved from the island of St. Helena to the church of the Invalides at Paris, and a tomb built at the expense of the State, the expedition commanded by His Royal Highness, the Prince de Joinville.'

On Sunday 18th, at eight o'clock, the ships were under sail,

* Naval commissioner Chèdeville has left some interesting documents: a water-colour of the body being handed over by General Middlemore to the Prince de Joinville on the quay at Jamestown and a pencil drawing of Longwood House transformed into a farm by its tenant during the years 1823–1840, both now in the Longwood Museum. As for Dr. Guillard, he was responsible for a charming sepia sketch of the embarkation of the sarcophagus on to *La Belle-Poule*, which is also at Longwood.

making to the north-north-west. When they were two miles from the island the *Oreste* turned and passed astern of *La Belle-Poule*, firing a salute of five guns before heading west towards Buenos Aires. The onlookers still collected on Jamestown quay heard *La Favorite* return the salute, and then saw the sails fade on the horizon to the north. The sea-girt mausoleum returned to its previous silence, while the body of the man they had treated as a pariah travelled in its sextuple coffin towards the sublime apotheosis of rediscovery.*

* *La Belle-Poule* also carried on board the flagstones which had covered the tomb. After lying forgotten in the arsenal at Cherbourg, they are now displayed at the Invalides along with other valuable relics of St. Helena, including the hearse used at the 1821 funeral, presented to Napoleon III by Queen Victoria.

VIII

THE EMPEROR AT THE INVALIDES

✳

For many hours the passengers on board *La Belle-Poule* could make out the dark irregular outline of the desolate rock on the grey horizon, with its crown of clouds and the colossal profile of the Emperor carved for eternity on the flanks of the mountain where wild goats lived, called the Barn. When that vision finally vanished like a bad dream, and the frigate was being propelled homewards by a gentle following wind, every face shone with satisfaction.

The Emperor's ex-companions thrilled with pleasure every time the boatswain blew his whistle and at every change of direction, for they felt proud to be bringing back to France, in the face of the whole world, the remains of the man whose misery and humiliations they had shared. Marchand was remembering as if it were yesterday the sound of the Emperor's voice growling wearily:

'You will return to Europe, you will rejoin your families there; your friends will gather round you and ask for the smallest details about my life on this miserable rock ... Montholon will find his wife and his children, you your mother, and I shall be dead, left behind in this melancholy solitude.'

To bring the body back from exile and escort it to the restorative pomp of a splendid funeral on the banks of the Seine was for the executors who had been his last confidants the only worthy end to their journey, and the crowning fulfilment of a supreme wish. In the ward-room and the crews' quarters many relics from St. Helena had been stacked – fragments of the first coffin,

willow branches, woodwork from Longwood House, earth from
the grave: never had a mission aroused such pride or inspired such
devotion. France was awaiting the Emperor's ashes; but they
were bringing her the miraculously preserved body of their
hero, and England, as if embarrassed by her memories, had given
to the dead the honours she had grudged to the living.

A shadow was cast across this picture on October 31, by a
merchant ship, bringing a Dutch gazette full of disturbing news
concerning affairs in the Levant. France had espoused the cause
of Mehemet Ali, Pasha of Egypt, against Turkey; England had
replied by forming an alliance with Austria, Prussia and Russia to
settle the Egyptian question. In Paris they were talking of a
'moral Waterloo' and were feverishly preparing for action to
wipe out the shame of 1815. Louis Philippe restrained to the
best of his ability the warlike enthusiasm of Thiers, who stormed
furiously: 'Louis Philippe is an intaglio; Napoleon was a cameo.'
On November 2 a schooner flying a Dutch flag confirmed the
fact that hostilities had broken out in the Mediterranean and the
chancelleries of Europe stood on the brink of war, the breach
between France and the four great powers having taken place.
Joinville was appalled at the thought of the danger to his precious
cargo should he be engaged by British ships, and decided to speed
full-sail to Cherbourg, abandoning *La Favorite*, whose slow
progress retarded them. Joinville wanted to take Marchand on
board, but had to leave him on *La Favorite* for lack of space, thus
depriving him of the spectacle of their arrival at Cherbourg. Also
on that ship was the body of Robert d'Harcourt, a young man
of nineteen, who died at St. Helena in April 1840 after having
been put off there by a French ship on which he was a passenger.
Foreseeing the worst, Joinville had the partitions removed between the cabins in use by members of the expedition, and all
their handsome furnishings thrown into the sea – thus allowing
the ship's batteries to go into action and *La Belle-Poule* to fire
all her guns; the shot-lockers were filled and battle-drills multi-
plied. If luck was against them, the ship would sink beneath the

waves with her crew, who would thus have the glory of sharing
the Emperor's last resting-place, rather than allow the corpse to be
taken from them.*

All went well, however, and the voyage passed without incident.
Indifferent to the noise of feet as the decks were cleared for action,
the Abbé Coquereau recited prayers for the dead every day at the
foot of the catafalque, and celebrated mass whenever the state of
the sea permitted. On the 10th the frigate crossed the tropic, on
the 18th she sighted Sainte-Marie of the Azores, and on Sunday
November 29 at six o'clock the look-out men signalled the
lighthouse and harbour lights of Cherbourg. Next morning, at
five o'clock, a favourable wind enabled Joinville to enter the roads
and penetrate the biggest dock without towing, greeted by salutes
from the batteries of Fort-Royal, Honnet and Querqueville.

Cherbourg owed its port and arsenal to Napoleon; several of its
inhabitants had watched them built, and this was a gala occasion
for the town: within one week more than 100,000 people went to
kneel beside the catafalque, now ornamented by a gold crown
voted by the town council.

In five months the political situation had changed, and since
November 26 poor Monsieur Thiers, who had been the architect
of the return of the ashes, was replaced at the head of the Cabinet
by Marshal Soult (Duc de Dalmatie by favour of Napoleon) while
Guizot was the eminence grise and the power behind the new
Cabinet. Warned of the arrival of the expedition by a dispatch
from Rohan-Chabot from Cherbourg, Soult had fixed the official
ceremony for December 15, and at eight o'clock in the morning
the coffin was placed on the deck of *La Belle-Poule*, be-flagged
for the occasion, for a last mass before transhipment to *La Normandie*, which would transport it as far as the mouth of the Seine.
Pouring rain disturbed the ceremony, which was witnessed by the
town authorities, clergy and populations massed on the quays,
while a thousand guns from all the forts and ships in the roadstead
saluted the Emperor's official arrival in his native land. With the

* These preparations and fears were gloated over later in London.

aid of a sloping bridge the catafalque was lowered on to *La Normandie* and placed on the quarter-deck, protected from the inclement weather by a dome supported by twelve columns and covered in embroidered velvet. There were a gilt cross and lamps on the altar at the foot of the mizzen-mast, and it was enhanced by silver eagles; the flag made by the ladies of St. Helena floated from the main-mast.

When the boat spouted smoke and beat the water with its paddle-wheels, the drums began to roll softly, the troops presented arms and flags were lowered. Joinville, his officers and the members of the expedition took their places on board, as did the band of *La Belle-Poule* and a hundred members of the crew. Two hundred more embarked on the steam-vessels *Le Véloce*, (Captain Martineng) and *Le Courrier* (Captain Gaubin) – one of them to salute land at the mouth of the Seine, the other as escort.

The sea was tranquil, and next day at six o'clock in the morning the convoy reached Le Havre, whose inhabitants were wild with excitement: 'Perhaps no event in history has been celebrated with the splendour accompanying the unhoped-for translation of the mortal remains of the Emperor Napoleon,' read a notice put up by the town prefect. 'You will pay this great man the last honours with that dignified calm appropriate to people who have so often felt the effects of his protective power and of his particular good-will.' In spite of the pale sunshine the temperature was freezing cold, and the windswept countryside was covered in hoar-frost. But Le Havre, like its prefect, remembered. Despite the earliness of the hour and the icy weather, the crowds massed along the quays round the civil authorities, clergy and soldiers of the National Guard. This was only the first of many splendid triumphal receptions. The convoy set off amid cheering and shouts, a scene which was to be repeated in every town, every village they passed through. Church bells tolled, and the inhabitants stood in groups behind their municipal officials, noisily expressing their joy.

As *La Normandie* could not take them up the Seine, the vessels were moored at Val-de-Lahaye, downstream from Rouen, for the night of the 9th to 10th, there to await the flotilla coming to convey them as far as Courbevoie: three *Dorades*, three *Etoiles*, *L'Elbeuvien*, *Le Parisien*, *La Parisienne* and *Le Lampa*. The catafalque travelled on the black-painted *Dorade 3*, under its pall of purple velvet decorated with gold bees and eagles, still guarded by Joinville, his officers, and the Emperor's ex-companions. *La Dorade* had at first been decked with garlands and draperies but Joinville decided: 'The boat shall be painted black; the coffin shall be in the bows covered with the funeral pall brought from St. Helena; the gentlemen of the mission at the corners; incense is to be burnt; the cross at the head; the priest shall stand in front of the altar; my aide-de-camp and I in the stern will announce that this boat bears the mortal remains of the Emperor.' Towards noon on the 10th they reached Rouen, with its quays swarming with sightseers. An arc de triomphe decorated with flags, fasces, and hangings stamped with the Emperor's arms (found perhaps in the lofts of the town hall) had been set up in the middle of the Seine under the suspension bridge ... Along the banks were pyramids bearing the names of the great victories of the Empire.

When *La Dorade 3* came to a stop under the arch, the whole flotilla dropped anchor and the clergy made ready for prayers of intercession. Cries of 'Hurrah for the Emperor' went up from the crowds of fully armed soldiers, peasants muffled up against the cold, and veterans of the Grande Armée, stamping to keep their feet warm as they had often done in the old days. The passengers of *La Dorade 3* were all in the same case: the poor wretches had to sleep on wooden benches in a cold of twelve degrees below zero. Bells rang and horses reared when the loud voices of cannon drowned their sound. In the suddenly ensuing silence the *De Profundis* rose aloft, punctuated every minute by the artillery on the heights of Sainte Catherine. A salute of a hundred guns followed the funeral service. As an eye-witness described it: 'All the signs of mourning disappeared, the church bells were in full peal, the drums beat out *Aux Champs*, the troops presented arms and the band played victory marches. Now Napoleon passed under the arc de triomphe raised in his honour by the good people of Rouen, and the veterans waiting impatiently on the bridge above threw down crowns of everlasting-flowers and branches of laurel.'

The same enthusiasm at Elbeuf, at Les Andelys, at Vernon and at Mantes, and then on the evening of the 12th the flotilla halted for the night at Poissy bridge, where they were to be guarded by troops of the line and the Garde Nationale, who had carefully prepared the Emperor's last bivouac. 'One could see the uniforms glowing in the torchlight; sentinels relieving each other and exchanging shouts; drums were beating the Reveille. It was still dark and if the Emperor were to have woken he could have believed he was sleeping in camp.'

Next day was Sunday and the Abbé Coquereau celebrated mass at ten o'clock. The young Duc d'Aumale had arrived from Paris and stood beside his brother, Joinville; the decks of the boats were full of sailors and on the banks fully armed troops surrounded the local clergy. Braving the icy gusts of wind, the people of Poissy and its environs stood shoulder to shoulder in an impressive silence. When the ceremony was over the convoy started off again towards Maison-sur-Seine, slowly filing past under the terrace of the Château de Saint-Germain, where the prefect did the honours, surrounded by the municipal authorities. At Saint-Denis the young ladies of the Legion of Honour were wearing mourning, and the canons sang the service for the dead as *La Dorade 3* went by, hidden in a tide of shivering, huddled humanity. This assiduity on the part of the clergy enraged the royalist clan, who combined hatred for the dead Bonaparte and for Louis Philippe as King: 'It's rather strange to see the populace kneeling round the clergy who are blessing this corpse, and wanting their hero to receive everywhere the benediction of the Church,' commented the Duchesse de Dino.

'If I ever needed a refuge, it is among the people of Paris that I would seek it,' Bonaparte had declared in 1800. There had in fact been established between this authoritarian conqueror and the gay city he had made the capital of Europe, a relationship as persistent and strong as great love. Napoleon had a high esteem for the humble folk whose cheering drowned the witty conversation of salons, and he was fond of repeating: 'My particular confidence in all classes of the people of the capital has no bounds.' The crowds in the streets had been put to every test yet their enthusiasm had not dwindled, and in June 1815 after the disaster of Waterloo, the populace had come beating in waves on the walls of the Elysée: their loyalty had not altered the balance of Destiny, and twenty-five years had passed, yet the same invisible force drove the flood towards the Seine, 'an ocean of men' said one of those present, who remembered.

The director of Fine Arts had entrusted to the Parisian undertakers the decoration of a boat-catafalque, a sort of floating funeral temple, supported by caryatids, heavily decorated with bronze gilt and draperies, on whose prow a large eagle with wings outspread seemed to be leading the convoy. The efforts of the director of Fine Arts were not approved by Alphonse Karr: 'On the whole the ceremony seems, from what I have read in the papers, to have been much too like an Olympic Circus. This will surprise no one when I say that the arrangements were entrusted to M. Cavé and three other light comedy friends of his. M. Cavé, director of the Beaux Arts, has written a vaudeville called *Vive* [*sic*] *la joie et les pommes de terre*.' This heavy vessel, painfully drawn along against the current, was in danger of slowing up progress, and Joinville preferred to keep the body on *La Doirade 3*: the splendid imperial boat therefore joined the rear of the flotilla, but empty, while a steamboat manoeuvred round to the head and two hundred musicians, perishing with cold, attacked the tunes specially composed for the occasion by Auber, Halévy and Adam.

That evening they reached Courbevoie, the terminus of the river voyage; troops of the line, National Guards, Parisians and old soldiers of the Empire all joined in a gigantic bivouac. It was freezing hard and a bitter wind fanned the great bonfires round which the old and footsore huddled together, with grim faces, to welcome their Emperor: they came and went silently, then, worn out with the nervous strain of waiting, rolled themselves up in their cloaks for the night in shapeless bundles. Perhaps the familiar bugle calls of Headquarters were echoing in their ears – the reveille, the March of the Consular Guard, or the rumpus of trumpets and drums which announced the arrival of the grey overcoat: *Pour l'Empereur* ... They seemed to see ghosts from that period of glory and misery that was their youth emerging from the shadows: riders whose mounts had galloped at Marengo, at Austerlitz and in the snows of Moscow, marshals in plumed hats coming away from the imperial tent, that holy of holies ...

'Soult,' said someone.

'Soult!' echoed the others.

It was indeed Soult, who had come to kneel at his sovereign's feet. The Duc de Dalmatie, Marshal of the Empire, closed his eyes and let his memories submerge him: the Consular Guard ... Austerlitz ... He heard the curt voice, on the evening of that great battle:

'Monsieur le Maréchal, you have covered yourself with glory.'

Jena, Eylau, Tilsitt, Spain, the victory over Wellington ... There was more than enough there to make a hero.

Huddled over the prie-dieu, insensible to the cold, he thought also of Louis XVIII's ministry, of the persecution of 'Bonaparte', of the word 'Usurper' so rashly bandied about ... It could not fail to bring tears to the eyes of a soldier at his rendezvous with the past.*

* * *

* Soult, Duc de Dalmatie (1769–1851), hero of Austerlitz, a name he nearly took in his title of duke; defeated at Toulouse in 1814, he went over at once to Louis XVIII, thus gaining the War Office – and made use of that promotion to penalise the Bonapartists heavily ... Reconciled with Napoleon during the Hundred Days and appointed chief of staff, he had to go into exile after Waterloo. Returning in 1819, he was made a peer of France in 1827. Secretary of State for War under Louis Philippe from 1830 to 1832, President of the Council in 1839 and 1840 to 1847, he was to become marshal-general of France in 1847.

Dawn broke on the 15th over this handful of ghosts who had refused the hospitality of the people of Courbevoie to watch all night, lying on the frozen ground as they had in Russia; there were several hundred of them, veterans of Egypt, Spain, Russia or the Isle of Elba, officers and soldiers in the uniform of the Guard, dignitaries and officials of the Empire, fighting against exhaustion and cold with fiercer strength than Louis Philippe's men, whose powers of endurance were failing. At eight o'clock stamping of feet and murmurs suddenly stopped, on the arrival of a broken old man in mourning, leaning on two younger men, who were as deeply moved as he was.

'Larrey!' said one old man in amazement.

'Larrey!' was taken up in chorus.

Larrey – the man of whom Napoleon wrote in his will: 'He is the most virtuous man I have ever known,' the surgeon-in-chief to the imperial armies, who had braved twenty-five campaigns, sixty battles and three wounds, to whom many wounded men owed their lives. His face was familiar to all those who had been under fire, from Egypt to Moscow, a face that was smiling and weeping at the thought of hobbling along behind the hearse of the hero of his life. Close behind him there came some huge fellows in great excitement; they were Polish delegates and were received by Bertrand and Gourgaud. General Ribinski, leader of the insurrection of 1831 for his country's independence, spoke for his companions, standing stiffly to attention in front of the members of the St. Helena expedition, and booming out:

'Faithful to honour and duty, the Poles who shared the glory and defeats of the French eagles have come to pay their last homage to the Emperor.' On April 8, 1814, General Krasinski, commanding the 1st Regiment of Light Horse Lancers, had written to Napoleon who had just abdicated: 'Some of your marshals have betrayed you, some of your generals have gone over to the enemy. The Poles will never betray you, Sire, while I am their leader.'

Magic of the past regained . . . The brave old man seemed to be waiting for an invisible hand to pinch his ear and for the familiar voice to utter the words:

'General, I am pleased with you.'

At about nine o'clock the sailors from *La Belle-Poule* lifted up the coffin, carried it on shore and placed it under an open Greek temple where the hearse was standing, drawn by sixteen black horses, harnessed four by four, and caparisoned in gold. On this heavy contraption weighing thirteen tons and ten metres high, was a cenotaph copied from the coffin, and supported by fourteen statues representing victories. Ornaments in profusion: spirits carrying Charlemagne's crown or blowing trumpets of fame, piles of arms, the imperial crown, sceptre and hand of justice, all glittering with precious stones, trophies in the shape of flags, palms and laurels. The coffin was not placed on top of this amazing construction, as the spectators believed, but in the undercarriage.

A cannonade of twenty-one guns from Neuilly and the Invalides shook the air as the hearse began to move, and this gave the signal for the great bells of Notre-Dame and the other churches to begin tolling. Ever since five o'clock Paris had been living in a fever of excitement over this historic occasion, and to the rhythm of the drums of the National Guard the crowd began hurrying towards the Avenue de Neuilly, by which the funeral cortège would arrive at the Arc de Triomphe. Although the temperature was fourteen degrees below zero, spectators stood admiring the group crowning the monument of victory, which was draped in festoons and garlands: it represented Napoleon in coronation robes, standing erect on a trophy made up of conquered weapons, and surrounded by the attributes of Victory. The group in question was a copy of one of the numerous projects for a crowning ornament to the monument that had been considered from 1825 to 1882 but never adopted. It was the work of Blouet. Different coloured flares were burning at the angles of the platform. At the four corners of the arch, symbols of Glory and Greatness had been erected.

Leaving Courbevoie at ten, the hearse only reached L'Etoile at half-past eleven. From the start the veterans of the Guard gave trouble by rebelling against the arrangements of the Minister of the Interior which placed them behind the general and town councillors of the commune.

'The organisers of the ceremony have forgotten that the Emperor always marched in the middle of his Guard!' they protested. 'The Guard has taken its proper place, and knows very well how to keep it.'

There was wrangling and jeering, and a general on horseback failed to bring these relics of past glory to heel, after which the old men formed into groups of twenty-five, each representing one regiment of the Guard, and consented to mingle with the rest, grumbling loudly at all these 'louis-philippards'.

The National Guard lined the streets. The Seine gendarmerie in their bearskin caps led the march, followed by the municipal guard on horseback, squadrons of lancers and General Darriule, commanding officer of the fortress of Paris. Next came a battalion of infantry with arms reversed, the municipal guard on foot, firemen, lancers, cuirassiers, and the chief of the military police, General Pajol (who had been in the cavalry under the Empire), followed by two hundred officers serving in Paris, Saint-Cyr and the Polytechnic, infantry, artillery, light infantry and engineers. Four squadrons of the National Guard on horseback, with flags and band, in blue uniforms with scarlet facings, preceded Marshal Gérard, commander-in-chief of the National Guard, former President of the Council and Louis Philippe's Minister for War. He was the hero of the battle of Ligny, and Napoleon said of him at St. Helena: 'He was one of my new marshals.' The National Guard of Paris and the suburbs passed slowly along with drums and bands, and after it came the black and silver carriage of the Abbé Coquereau, followed by a group of senior naval officers, officers on the reserve or retired, and a band playing funeral music.

'The Emperor's horse!' murmured the shivering crowd.

It was, or rather was made out to be, Napoleon's battle charger: on his back was the saddle used by the First Consul, of maroon velvet embroidered with gold, the saddle-cloth, holsters, bit and stirrups ornamented with silver-gilt. The animal was caparisoned with violet crêpe sprinkled with gold bees. He seemed terrified, and was in fact a horse from the Parisian undertakers. His feebleness aroused Madame de Chateaubriand's pity: 'Nothing could have been sadder than a poor old lame horse snatched from the knacker to come and play Bucephalus to the great man, nor more touching than the tears that nine degrees of frost made to flow from everyone's eyes.'

Twenty-four non-commissioned officers wearing medals preceded the carriage of the members of the mission to St. Helena, including Rohan-Chabot and Gourgaud, who received an ovation; thirty-four more marched in front of the marshals of France and the eighty-seven flags of the departments of Algeria.

'Long live Joinville!' shouted the spectators. 'Hurrah for *La Belle-Poule!*'

The young Prince, surrounded by his staff officers, was at the head of his sailors, who marched in two lines escorting the hearse. The Pall was carried by Lieutenant-General Bertrand, Marshals Molitor and Oudinot (Grand Chancellor of the Legion of Honour) and Admiral Roussin.*

---

* Molitor (1770–1849). A volunteer in 1791 he was a general by 1800 and distinguished himself at Wagram. Louis XVIII made him inspector of the infantry of Metz in 1814. He rallied to Napoleon during the Hundred Days and after Waterloo incurred royal disgrace. Reinstated some years later, in 1823 he fought in Spain, where he got his marshal's baton.

Oudinot (1767–1847). National Guard during the Revolutionary period, then Lieutenant-Colonel of the Volunteers of the Meuse in 1791, General in 1794, many times wounded. He commanded the grenadiers of the Grande-Armée, was made marshal of France after Wagram and then Duc de Reggio. Peer of France under Louis XVIII, he held aloof from the Emperor during the Hundred Days, and the second Restoration saw him commanding the National Guard. Louis Philippe appointed him Grand Chancellor of the Legion of Honour and in 1842 governor of the Invalides.

Roussin (1781–1854) distinguished himself during the expedition to Ireland.

The survivors of the Imperial Household marched behind the catafalque with their eyes fixed on the statues of victories carrying their sovereign to his last home. It is said that Montholon, in prison in the fortress of Ham with Prince Louis, had requested twenty-four hours of liberty to be present at the ceremony, promising on his honour to return to prison the same evening. 'It was impossible to refuse,' states Alphonse Karr. 'They refused.'

Next came the Prefect of the Seine, Rambuteau, former Chamberlain to the Emperor, the prefect of Police and the members of the general council, at whose heels followed amazing figures. There were shouts of:

'Hurrah for the Guard!'

Here they were, in fact, the grenadiers, light infantry, mamelukes and riflemen of the Old Guard, the Empress' dragoons, hussars, guides and red lancers: threadbare overcoats, tarnished braid, shapeless shakos and caps, worn-down heels, not so long ago sticky with the mud of Austerlitz, the Beresina or Waterloo. Behind them filed the legions of the National Guard, dragoons, generals and field-marshals, artillery and infantry – but it was *they*, with their old-fashioned uniforms, faded bearskin bonnets and soiled red ribbons, *they* were the ones to close this chapter of history. Deeply moved, the crowd chanted 'Long live the Guard,' naming them as they passed, just as if they were returning from places with names like Wagram or the Beresina; but *they*, walking side by side, with inscrutable faces, seemed to be seeing with the eyes of memory beyond the gilt-covered bulk rolling over the paving-stones and beyond the heads of the crowd, the figure of Le Tondu, riding under the Arch of Carrousel on his white horse.

Along the Champs-Elysées with its decorations of twelve victories draped in flags, columns, urns of fire and eagles cut from

---

After devoting himself to hydrography, he was made Peer of France and ambassador at Constantinople before being named Minister for the Navy by Thiers in 1840, and by Guizot in 1843.

gilt cardboard, not a window was shut, not a balcony was empty, and there were hangings everwhere. One house had set up rows of seats at 10 or 5 francs each. There was a balcony to let for 3,000 francs or a dormer window for 50. Victor Hugo saw a hussar of the Guard in his old blue dolman, red trousers, and sabretache, who might have walked out of a museum of costumes, as he passed the crowd yelling 'Hurrah for the Emperor!' Street vendors were selling the programme of what they irreverently called 'The Festival of the Ashes', ballads, coloured prints, and souvenirs of the legend such as pipes and snuff-boxes bearing the unforgettable profile. Omnibuses packed with people were circulating through the neighbouring streets covered in streamers announcing 'To Napoleon's funeral at the Invalides'. Clusters of street-arabs were hanging from the trees and shaking down the hoar-frost covering them. In such a mob everything could hardly be expected to go smoothly, and the shouts of those who thought they had been given bad places were echoed by hostile cries such as 'Down with Guizot! Down with the ministers! Down with the English!' Foreign ambassadors *en poste* in Paris, having decided not to attend the ceremony, gathered at the English and Russian embassies, protected by military guards. From the balcony of the fine private house which stood at the corner of the rue de la Charte (today rue de la Boëtie) and the Champs-Élysées, Madame de Flahaut (whose husband was following the coffin among a group of aides-de-camp) stood shivering among some old friends – Maréchale Ney, the Duchesse de Rovigo and the Duchesse d'Albuféra. The ladies rejoiced to hear the crowd shouting: 'Hurrah for Napoleon!' Madame de Flahaut was Scottish, being the daughter of that same Lord Keith who received the *Bellerophon* at Plymouth in 1815. She kept repeating to her guests that her husband served the First Consul at the age of fifteen, that he fought at Friedland and at Wagram, and that after Waterloo he had not deserted the Emperor in the dark hours of defeat and panic. 'Something great and good must have been in this man, something loving and kindly, that has kept his name so cherished in the popular memory and gained him such a lasting love and affection,' wrote Thackeray who was present.

A salute of twenty-one cannon now announced that the Emperor was lying under the Arc de Triomphe beneath stones that recounted the stages in his career. Next came the triumphal descent of the Avenue and across the Place de la Concorde, disfigured by gigantic statues representing Wisdom, Strength, Justice and War or the Fine Arts and Eloquence, regardless of order. A massive cry of 'Hurrah for the Emperor' was soon drowned by the cannon from the Invalides. The hearse passed before other statues: kings from Clovis to Louis XIV, great soldiers, from Ney, Condé, MacDonald, Charles-Martel and La Tour d'Auvergne to Duguesclin and Joan of Arc, all surrounded by flares with snow whirling in their light.

On the Esplanade more than 40,000 guests of the government and of the two Chambers were massed on banks of seats beneath a timid sun which emerged from the clouds at the very moment when the panting horses drew the hearse to a halt in front of the Invalides. The iron gate was draped with black hangings fixed to tall columns and fastened by fasces, and so was the gateway into the main courtyard. Six thousand guests sat shivering on ranks of seats. The King and Queen, who had arrived about noon with the whole court, were waiting in a deconsecrated chapel, where the cold was glacial and the chimneys smoked so badly that everyone's eyes were watering. Louis Philippe was wearing the braided uniform of a lieutenant-general, and the Queen, who was unwell, wore deep mourning as did her daughters-in-law.

The nave had filled up, and ministers and the royal family had taken their seats, when thirty sailors from *La Belle-Poule* handed over the coffin to non-commissioned officers, who carried it to the gateway, stooping under its weight. A triumphant funeral march began as the Archbishop of Paris and his clergy arrived in a procession, received the body and entered the church followed by a cortège headed by Bertrand, quite broken and weak with emotion. Louis Philippe descended from his throne and took a few steps. Joinville stood to attention and saluted him with his sword.

'Sire, I present you with the body of the Emperor Napoleon.'

'I receive it in the name of France,' replied the King simply.

Such at least was the *Moniteur's* version. In his *Souvenirs*, Joinville later wrote: 'It seems that the Council had composed a little speech for me to deliver when I met my father and the reply he should have made to it. Only they had forgotten to inform me. So on arriving I merely gave the salute with my sword and retired. After a moment of hesitation, my father improvised a conventional phrase, and the *Moniteur* arranged matters afterwards.'

Soult presented the King with a sword, and Louis Philippe handed it to Bertrand.

'General, I charge you to place the Emperor's sword on his coffin.'

With his face wet with tears, Bertrand came forward like someone in a dream, as if he heard his sovereign's voice in his ears saying: 'One day you will again hear Paris shout "Long live the Emperor!"'

'General Gourgaud, place the Emperor's hat on the coffin.'

This was the cocked hat Napoleon had worn at Eylau; beside it was laid the cross of the Legion of Honour. To make room for the catafalque the altar had had to be taken away; as Thackeray remarked sarcastically 'And why not? Who is God here but Napoleon?'

The Archbishop of Paris and four bishops read the prayers of intercession, and then the service began; the Communion of Martyrs lasted two hours and was followed by Mozart's Requiem sung by some of the greatest singers of the time, including Grisi and Duprez, accompanied by a choir of six hundred. Berlioz didn't appreciate the choice of music: 'Oh! Our sublime emperor, what a pitiful reception they gave him. My tears froze under the lids more with shame than cold ... Mozart's *Requiem* made a pretty poor effect, even if it is a masterpiece; its proportions are not appropriate to such a ceremony.' The hubbub from the crowd collected in the courtyard, all trying to make their way into the sanctuary, at times drowned the voices of the officiating clergy, and some ministers were chattering together with complete lack of manners ... Opposite the court party, Marshal Moncey, governor of the Invalides, sat hunched in his chair: he was eighty-six and had been near his end for several weeks; every day he had said to his doctor:

'Doctor, keep me alive a little longer. I want to receive the Emperor.'

His eyes rested on the violet hangings embroidered with gold bees ... What memories they aroused in the mind of the doyen of the marshals! The attempt in the rue Saint-Nicaise, the arrest of the Duc d'Enghien, the Pichegru affair ... Life was not a bed of roses for the foremost gendarme of the Empire. Then came the command in Spain and the battles of 1814 to defend the threatened capital.

Napoleon used to say of Moncey: 'He's an honest man.'

His honesty had landed the marshal in prison at the time of Ney's condemnation, but fate had reserved for him the supreme reward of receiving the Emperor's body. The ceremony over, at about four o'clock, he sighed to the soldiers who carried his arm-chair.

'Now let's go home and die.'*

* * *

* Moncey (1754–1842). From general of the Revolution, the First Consul had made him inspector of the gendarmerie, and the Emperor Marshal of France and Duc de Conegliano after the Spanish campaign. Moncey again distinguished himself during the defeats of the Russian campaign, and at the barrier at Clichy. Created peer by Louis XVIII, and confirmed as such by Napoleon during the Hundred Days, his refusal to preside over the council of war to judge Marshal Ney after Waterloo gained him three months imprisonment in the fortress of Ham. After being freed he went to fight in Spain for the King. In 1833 Louis Philippe appointed him govenor of the Invalides.

The church was thrown open to the public for three weeks, and more than 100,000 persons filed past the coffin, some patiently waiting from ten in the morning until midnight in spite of the freezing cold. There were crowds too pressing round the hearse on view at the Arc de Triomphe, and on the banks of the Seine, which was frozen over, to gaze at the floating catafalque. 'If the exhibition had gone on any longer,' wrote one witness, 'people would have hurried from every other country to pay homage to the Emperor's mortal remains.' Soult gave a dinner for the members of the St. Helena commission. The King received the officers and crew of *La Belle-Poule*. The Abbé Coquereau was made Chevalier of the Legion of Honour. On December 18 the officers of the Guard gave a banquet to Horace Vernet and drank a toast to the Emperor on their knees.

As he came away from the ceremony Viennet gossiped with some of the peers.*

'It's more than the glorification of a great man,' grumbled one, 'it's like the restoration of his dynasty.'

'It's a fortunate day for the prisoner of Ham,' said another.

Only the King and the man-in-the-street were congratulating themselves on this return, on this avalanche of prayers, music and gilt papier mâché. 'And be sure of this, that as his Majesty Louis Philippe took his night-cap off his royal head that morning, he prayed heartily that he might, at night, put it on in safety,' was the comment of the English humorist Thackeray.†

Napoleon had seen Paris again and Paris had seen Napoleon without the slightest incident, and Guizot, who had haggled over all the display and opted for a purely military ceremony, to glorify the leader of men rather than the statesman, rubbed his hands at the thought of decking the July Monarchy with plumes from the

---

* Viennet (1777–1868) an old soldier of the Empire, and afterwards liberal deputy, in 1827 he was created peer of France by Louis Philippe. He has left essays, poems, novels, tragedies, plays and fables, but posterity remembers hardly anything of them but their titles.

† Thackeray was born in Calcutta and on his return to England in 1817 to go to boarding-school his ship put in at St. Helena. *The Roundabout Papers*.

eagle. Hadn't the spectators gone off to their streets or suburbs, arm in arm singing Henri Monnier's verses:

> 'Ami certain de la valeur
> Fidèle amant de la victoire,
> Il eut pour marraine la gloire
> et pour père le champ d'honneur.'

And a few weeks later didn't the Cirque Olympique, with the blessing of the censorship, put on an imposing spectacle consisting of five tableaux, with characters called Bertrand, Gourgaud, Montholon and Las Cases, set at St. Helena, on board *La Belle-Poule* and with a finale depicting the Parisian triumph?

But the sumptuous and interminable procession had disrupted the life of the capital: waves of people from all the suburbs had broken dangerously over the banks of the Seine as in the great days of the past, to commune with the Parisians in a cult of memory, with a fervour that shocked several royalists and surprised more than one foreigner.

The Comte de Ségur and the Comte Alfred de Montesquiou, two sons of the old monarchist régime who had gone over to the Empire, were to be seen walking side by side in the freezing mists of Courbevoie with anonymous veterans from the battalion of the Isle of Elba. A peer of France was seen buttoned into a uniform from Waterloo. A soldier disabled at Austerlitz was seen being carried by young men. Victor Hugo was seen, perched on a wooden dais, intoxicated by the spectacle he had foretold in alexandrines:

'Sire, vous reviendrez dans votre capital.'

Gérard, a marshal of France, had been seen proceeding down the Avenue at the head of a party of National Guards, and people reminded each other that if Grouchy had listened to that rough soldier the battle of Waterloo would have been a victory for Napoleon. The crowd had been seen to greet with as much affection as respect men who had been Napoleon's marshals, generals, aides-de-camp, chamberlains or equerries. Travelling coffee-sellers had been seen pouring their wares into receptacles draped in crêpe. Thousands of young people had been heard shouting 'Hurrah for the Emperor!' though they had known neither the Empire nor its leader.

The uproar had risen up as high as the salons where the royalists, to whom Bonaparte and Louis Philippe were both impostors, were peering out from behind their curtains and making fun of the 'ridiculous' decorations and the 'indecent' excitement, and repeating with pleasure the witticism of a legitimist: 'All these emotions dragged out of the old wardrobes of the Empire can't possibly survive fresh air.' It had risen also into rooms where people cherished Napoleon's memory as fervently as they mourn someone they revere. No one there was allowed to snigger at threadbare mamelukes, emaciated half-pay officers and limping veterans of Waterloo. Bonapartist ladies, 'the old female relics of the Empire' as Talleyrand's niece described them, were grouped round Madame de Flahaut, and trembled with hope when they heard the voice of the people (which is often that of history) make them the reparation that governments had refused them. Street vendors shouted the title of their pamphlet, in a maliciously deformed version: 'Description of the hearse and of those who betrayed it.'*

There were some alarmists and grumblers who hoped that the acclamations from the streets would be drowned in the sound of gunpowder. Two months earlier the fanatical Darmès, 'exterminator of tyrants', had fired at the King as he returned to Saint-Cloud accompanied by the Queen and Madame Adélaide: only two footmen and one National Guard had been wounded, but the rifle-shot had started a panic in the country and proved fatal to a Cabinet incapable of keeping public order. Thiers was replaced by Marshal Soult and François Guizot. The latter, whom Parisians had called, 'the man of Ghent' ever since Louis XVIII took refuge there during the Hundred Days, he was a careerist

* (Trahi = betrayed, trainé = pulled. Translator's note).

concealing his game successfully under a mask of cold austerity; he had enjoyed favour under the Empire without rendering 'unto Caesar the things which are Caesar's' in other words without even esteeming Napoleon. 'He who has received the Emperor's remains,' wrote *Le Courrier Français* 'was a man of the Restoration, one of those drawing-room conspirators who shook hands with the king of Ghent behind the English legions, while our old soldiers were getting killed in defence of their country in the plains of Waterloo.'

If there was a shortage of official ardour, what must be said about the material preparations? It was here that M. Thiers had shown a lack of authoritative and infectious enthusiasm. Here again Alphonse Karr strikes the right note: 'Destiny had amused herself by uniting in power a crowd of men who had betrayed the Emperor in his time, and had treated him fairly badly both in actions and writing.' In that circle there might be little or much enthusiasm so long as it was to order. Nothing was ready in the capital when *La Belle-Poule* dropped anchor in Cherbourg roads, and Napoleon's body remained in port for eight days; on the very morning of the Parisian apotheosis, the plaster of the monumental statue opposite the Dome still looked damp. When such details as these were revealed some laughed and others flew into a rage, and every time a voice shouted 'Hurrah for the Emperor!' there was someone else who wondered if this was not the signal for a movement to dismiss Guizot and bring back Thiers, or overthrow Louis Philippe and install that Prince Louis Napoleon at the Tuileries, who had just been imprisoned at Ham . . . In governmental circles Thiers was undoubtedly the man most to be feared, Thiers who was chafing as he watched a triumphant display he had instigated himself, and from which he had hoped to gain glory, and who smiled when he heard shouts of 'Down with Guizot! Down with the English! Down with the men of Ghent!'

Joinville and his sailors had certainly changed the situation by winning the approbation of this overcharged city. His expression was serious but he responded enthusiastically to the cheering; his weather-beaten crew were obviously proud of having escorted the body all the way from the depths of Geranium Valley into this blaze of national recognition.

'Long live Joinville!' shouted Paris wholeheartedly.

But when they saw the survivors from the past, bent, broken and limping along in their pitifully shabby uniforms, one cry drowned all the rest:

'Long live the Guard!'

The procession had ended in an atmosphere of genuine emotion which had driven away evil thoughts, yet Joinville had declared with a certain bitterness: 'Everything coming from the people is large-hearted, everything from the government is petty.' This stern criticism was aimed at those responsible for the Parisian festivities: the staff of the Invalides, under orders from the Minister of the Interior and controlled by Cavé, director of Fine Arts, helped by the architects Visconti and Labrouste, had created something with a savour of operatic decor. On the morning of December 15 the scaffoldings from the Paris undertakers were still cluttering the façade of the monument and the inside of the chapel of the Invalides. There was chaos during the period of waiting imposed on the officials by the time-table: the National Guard had picnicked in the arcades, street vendors plied their trade at doors where only those with invitation cards could enter, whereas no seats were reserved for the Invalides themselves. 'No one was thinking about the Emperor. People talked about everything under the sun except him,' said Madame Mollien, wife of the former head of the Treasury, who had become lady-in-waiting to Queen Marie-Amélie.

The marvel was that the government had escaped from this hornet's nest with so little damage, and that the crowd had been content with singing the *Marseillaise* and Monnier's verses with somewhat menacing ardour, and with breaking Guizot's windows at the Ministry for Foreign Affairs. Madame Mollien expressed the feelings of the whole court when she said to a friend on December

16: 'Everyone is delighted to have reached yesterday's tomorrow.'*

But what a tomorrow for the future and for history!

An enemy of the Empire, Apponyi, Austrian ambassador in Paris, had been terrified by the wild excitement of the populace. 'The wide Avenue of the Champs-Élysées was like an eddying, swirling torrent. Nothing could have withstood the impetuous curiosity of this moving mass ... Everything was turned upside down, invaded and crushed beneath ten times ten thousand feet – men's, women's and children's – which made as it were a single body with a thousand eyes.' What more would he have said had he known that some legions of the National Guard had joined with the crowd in booing ministers? He would not have blamed the Queen for being so afraid of an attempt on the King's person that she had kept close to his side from start to finish of this alarming day.

Alphonse Karr lifted the veil covering official hypocrisy:† 'I would like to believe in the pious regrets of King Louis Philippe, of M. Soult – soldier under the Empire – and of a crowd of others; but I am sure that they fell far short of those they would have felt if the Emperor had risen alive from his coffin and said "Here I am!"'

---

* However, in May 1840, it had been decided that the return of the ashes should coincide with the opening of the Chambers in December, so as to stifle 'all rumours or talk of ministerial changes, such as always arose from the floor of parliament at that season,' according to Joinville.

† Alphonse Karr gaily describes how the pseudo battle-charger went down to posterity: 'The day after the ceremony, four Englishmen, one of them a painter, appeared at the undertaker's office and asked to see the Emperor Napoleon's battle-charger. The horse had now returned to private life and gone out on business. Harnessed to another it was conveying a sixty-year-old virgin to the cemetery de l'Ouest, on the way to have her ancient virtue rewarded in heaven. The foreigners were told that the horse was tired and perhaps even moved by yesterday's ceremony and was not at home that day, but they could come back next day. Next day they were shown the animal, well wrapped up in flannel. They drew it from the side, the front, from behind, three-quarters, in every possible way, then they left for London where they were to produce a book on the Emperor's funeral, figuring the battle-charger.'

IX

THE OTHER NAPOLEON

❋

As they walked by the Invalides, certain deeply impressed passers-by may have said, like Don Carlos before Charlemagne's tomb:

'Oh dark Sepulchre
How can you contain, without breaking, so great a shade?'

Others, although constantly dreaming of the France of their youth and contrasting the great things they had done and the resounding triumphs they had witnessed with the greyness of the present day, denounced the return of the hero into Louis Philippe's Paris. Old and disappointed though he was, Chateaubriand found fresh ardour with which to summon up the image of the man who had been the great passion of his life, and indiscriminately condemned Thiers' initiative, the formality of the ceremony and the choice of a place of burial: 'Robbed of his catafalque among the rocks, Napoleon has come here to lie among the refuse of Paris. Instead of the ships which used to salute the second Hercules on his Mount Etna, the washerwomen of Vaugirard will loiter past with pensioners unknown to the Grande Armée.' Vigny tuned his lyre to the same refrain: 'Providence placed his ashes on a rock like Prometheus, beneath a willow like Jean-Jacques Rousseau, with the Atlantic Ocean enclosing His monument, out of reach of rioting and political conflict, on a volcano as extinct as the Revolution which gave birth to him.' The Rhinelander Heine, dazzled long ago by the sculptured majesty of Napoleon's entry into Dusseldorf as a conqueror, closed his book of recollections sadly: 'The Emperor is dead. With him the last of the heroes in the antique style is no more, and the new world of tradesmen can breathe at its ease, as though freed from some brilliant nightmare.' But Hugo was less categorical – he was in favour at court and smiled on the Academy which was to welcome him a month later – his contribution was a simple official stanza:

'Ciel glacé, soleil pur. – Oh! brille dans l'histoire
Du funèbre triomphe impérial flambeau.
Que le peuple à jamais te garde en sa mémoire
Jour beau comme la gloire
Froid comme le tombeau.'*

Then suddenly in 1845 Armand Lefebvre, diplomat and son of a diplomat, published his *History of the Emperor's cabinets during the Consulate and the Empire*, to prove that the state of France made the *coup d'état* of 18 Brumaire necessary and salutary: the door was thus laid open to quasi-unconditional admiration, such as impregnated Thiers' great work in twenty volumes, which began appearing that same year.

Like Michelet a master of admirably clear historical narrative, able to draw in many sources and conversations – he had known many important persons of the period – as well as on the archives of ministries (Foreign Affairs, Finance, War and the Interior), rich in political experience, an astonishingly gifted realist, expert in financial matters tactics and diplomacy, outstandingly intelligent, Thiers creates in his History a frieze sculptured in faultless marble yet quivering with life. For he was in possession of the necessary facts to present 'an exact and complete exposition of events as

---

*Casimir Delavigne published a poem one verse of which ended:
'La France reconnut sa face respectée
Même par le ver du tombeau.'
(France recognised that face, respected even by the worms of the tomb)
which inspired the savage comment from Alphonse Karr in his usual style:
'It is generally regretted that M. Delavigne's verses didn't follow the example of this well brought up worm.'
(Translator's note: 'vers' = poetry, 'ver' = worm.)

they actually happened'. Amongst this abundance of figures stands out the monumental statue of Napoleon as 'wisdom incarnate', endowed with a genius made for France, just as France's dynamism was made for him.

From his prison at Ham, Prince Louis listened with delight to this outburst of prose and poetry: he clung to the hope that time was on his side, and that Louis Philippe, Guizot and Thiers would shorten his time of waiting. He had good reasons to smile as he read the Paris news-sheets. During a whole year the Cirque Olympique advertised *Prince Eugène and the Empress Josephine*, eighteen tableaux, in the course of which the audience saw the distribution of the eagles, the great battles, St. Helena, and applauded the scene where Napoleon was enthroned in the Olympus of the Brave. On May 25, 1845, Prince Louis managed to escape from his guards disguised as a bricklayer called Badinguet and took refuge in London, whence he wrote to the French government that he had left prison without the slightest intention 'of becoming involved in politics, nor yet of trying to disturb the peace Europe was enjoying at present'. At the same time he slipped a note to one of his relations: 'Because my luck has betrayed me twice my Destiny is all the more certain to be fulfilled. I am waiting.' How right he was!

Everything concerning the Bonaparte family was now of interest to Parisians. When King Jérôme was intriguing to get leave to live in France, Victor Hugo announced to the astonished peers: 'I am musing on the great events of the past, and I am sometimes tempted to say to the Chamber, to the press, to the whole of France: Let us talk about the Emperor for a little, it will do us good.' That was in 1847, and the July Monarchy was approaching the abyss under the dull gaze of a seventy-five-year-old King.

On February 22, 1848, threatening rumbles were heard in Paris, and on the 24th Louis Philippe abdicated. The way was now clear, and on the morning of the 26th Prince Louis arrived in the capital and wrote to the provisional government: 'I hasten back from exile to take my place under the flag of the Republic.' He chose his moment well ... He was asked to leave, and did so, protesting the republican purity of his intentions. He went back to his rooms in London and went on waiting.

With that element of obstinacy that gave his character strength, he was convinced that a republic would be firmly established and that he would then be allowed to install himself in France as an ordinary citizen, or else that unrest would break out and give him the opportunity to present himself once more – this time to the people. At the elections of June 1848, without even putting himself up as a candidate, he was elected for the departments of Seine, Yonne, Charente-Maritime and Corsica, but he declined the honour when he learned that the provisional government was determined to arrest him as soon as he appeared at the frontier. In September, after the horrors of June had sealed the fate of the 1848 Republic, he was candidate in a by-election, without having been entered on any list or being a resident in France, without even legally possessing French nationality.* He was again chosen by five departments: Seine, Corsica, Charente-Inférieure, Moselle and Yonne. 'This is not the return of a prince,' said Victor Hugo jubilantly, 'but of an idea. His candidacy dates from Austerlitz.'

On September 26 he presented himself at the Palais Bourbon, and took his seat on a bench on the left to hear himself confirmed as member for Yonne; then he climbed the tribune and declared with an awkwardness that may have been assumed: 'no one is more devoted than I am to the defence of order and the strengthening of the republic.' In December 1848, 'citizen Napoleon Bonaparte' was elected President of the French Republic, and his first action on installing himself at the Elysée was to retire into the Silver Room, where in June 1815 his uncle had signed his act of abdication.

Time passed, and the situation was consolidating; in 1852 the

---

* He had become a citizen of the Canton of Thurgau in 1832, and had served in the Swiss artillery.

Code Civil became the Code Napoleon once more, a few months before the Prince-President became Emperor of the French after a referendum which gave him a majority of 96 per cent. On December 2, the anniversary of Austerlitz, the new Emperor made his entry into the capital wearing a general's uniform.*

Thus this man whom his enemies took for an imbecile, a Diafoirus, a lout or a cretin, had firmly but patiently controlled the course of events ... His name alone had forced the issue. Guizot was stunned: 'How astonished a man of sense would be today, who, after having slept the sleep of Epimenides since that day (1840), awoke to see the Prince on the French throne.' There were some incredulous witnesses to his triumph however: 'Prince Louis!' laughed Alphonse Karr. 'Let him be a deputy since enough electors voted for him; but to be afraid of him and credit him with the power to create another 18 Brumaire and take his uncle's place – really! The people are sensible enough to talk of "Napoleon" and "the Bonaparte family". The Empire is a glorious parenthesis in our history, but it is closed.'

*   *   *

It was impossible not to notice that Louis Bonaparte's rise coincided with the publication in September 1848 of that key-work, *Mémoires d'Outre-Tombe*. Chateaubriand had died on July 4, and visitors who came to show their respects to his remains, especially Victor Hugo, had paid less attention to the bunch of verbena laid on his pall by Juliette Récamier than to the padlocked deal box standing at the foot of the bed and containing the manuscript of his masterpiece.

'Bonaparte and I, two unknown sub-lieutenants,' the irrepressible René had written with that trace of pride characteristic of his genius ... memories of the marvellous nights of his youth in America, of his worldly and diplomatic triumphs, of agonising

* Ten years earlier, however, Heinrich Heine had written: 'The Empire is dead, and so is the Emperor; they have just been buried together in the Invalides.'

love-affairs grew blurred ... When the manuscript was revised after the July Revolution, Louis XVIII, Charles X and Madame Récamier, love and legitimacy all gave way in nearly every chapter to Napoleon, who hovered over the work like Fate. At his first interview, Bonaparte 'noticed' young Chateaubriand, and 'recognised' him without knowing him. 'Since then,' confessed the writer in 1838, when nearly seventy, 'my days have been nothing but a series of visions'. But by ordering the execution of the Duc d'Enghien Bonaparte drove Chateaubriand into the ranks of discontent and then of opposition (in spite of Elisa Bacchiochi's protection), and finally made an enemy of him by refusing him the foremost places. Since nothing escaped the sharp eyes of the new master of France, the writer had been banished (a fairly mild punishment), to his comfortable house in the Vallée-aux-Loups after his provocative article of 1807 in the *Mercure*: 'In vain does Nero flourish, Tacitus is already born within the Empire.' After publishing *Les Martyrs* he was elected to the Académie Française with the Emperor's consent ('this constant mixture of anger and attraction Bonaparte feels for me is very strange'), and the speech he wrote for his reception was a provocative text, which 'had it been uttered would have closed the doors of the Institute to me and thrown me into the deepest of dungeons for the rest of my life'.

But surely Napoleon's tyranny was more bearable for a man of genius than the indifference or even ingratitude of the Bourbons, who had learnt nothing and forgotten nothing? Chateaubriand had believed himself 'necessary' to the Restoration, yet Louis XVIII had deprived him of his pension as Minister of State and then dismissed him from the Ministry of Foreign Affairs. At odds with the July Monarchy, in the evening of his days, he plunged bitterly into the memoirs which have given us the history of a whole century.

A lonely, monolithic character, proud of his reputation and intoxicated with his own intransigence, as he bent over the turbulent past he found only one human being measuring up to his standard – Napoleon. Was this really a literary strategem to conciliate a generation infatuated with the legend and its future? Sainte-Beuve thought so: 'He saw too late that he had attacked and insulted that great popular idol, Napoleon. He wanted to conciliate everyone, to make amends.' Is it not simpler to imagine that when the time came to shut away into their wooden box the pages that were to survive him, it seemed to him essential to confess to an admiration he had formerly rejected on principle or through disappointment?

*   *   *

The shadow of St. Helena hovered over the newborn Empire, and in 1853 a commission ordered to examine into the execution of the Emperor's will, presided over by Comte d'Ornano, governor of the Invalides, informed Napoleon III that the last wishes of the founder of his dynasty had been 'imperfectly carried out', the legatees having only received half the sums due to them and those named in the codicils nothing at all, and that a definitive settlement would be an act of 'national dignity'. To indemnify the former and do honour to the rest, such as those wounded at Waterloo, or the town of Brienne, the commissioners asked for 8,000,000 francs. On May 6 the settlement of the exile's posthumous debts had been completed: the descendants of Bertrand, (dead in 1844), received 522,967 francs, of Montholon (dead in 1853) 667,282 francs, and Marchand got 213,980 francs.

An Empire reborn from its ashes by the sole means of the magic virtue of the name of Napoleon was also in honour bound to give pledges to the rest of Europe, which had not forgotten . . . England in particular, powerful and touchy, would naturally show some repugnance at seeing a nephew of 'Bonaparte' on the throne of the Tuileries. By a strange reversal of fate, it was England who stood surety for the régime: Palmerston, still Foreign Secretary, recognised the *coup* of December 2 without even referring the matter to the Prime Minister and his colleagues in the Cabinet, and

Her Britannic Majesty's ambassador presented his credentials on December 5. This gesture greatly relieved the new sovereign, who was firmly bent on maintaining amicable relations with Great Britain, at the cost of soon being taxed with anglomania. An anglomaniac he probably was, for he remembered that he had been well-received in London during the difficult times of exile: his reticence and his caustic humour had been appreciated, and his blue eyes and strange smile had gained him more than one conquest. He had been a member of the exclusive Carlton Club, he had dressed with studied elegance and owned some fine horses. It was said that he had belonged to a masonic lodge and that he had enjoyed the favours of a wealthy Miss Howard, but this was all part of a gentlemanly way of life, and Queen Victoria herself remembered affectionately the Bonaparte who spoke English with a drawling accent, like Prince Albert's, and although she judged womanisers so harshly that she refused him the hand of one of her nieces, Princess Adelaide of Hohenlohe-Langenburg, just as she refused another niece, Princess Mary of Cambridge, to King Jérôme's son, it was agreed that the two courts should exchange official visits in 1855. Napoleon III and the Empress went to London in April, and Victoria and Albert risked a visit to Paris in August: no legitimate British sovereign had appeared in the capital since the coronation of Henry VI in 1431 . . .

Everything went off perfectly. There were cries of 'Long live the Queen of England!' At the station, Napoleon III presented his cousin, Prince Napoleon, who made a poor impression. (King Jérôme, his father, was sulking at Le Havre, having refused to give precedence to Prince Albert, and as Napoleon's brother declining the honour of 'welcoming that Queen'). One of the members of the royal suite found that this Bonaparte looked like 'a shabby bass-singer of some obscure Italian theatre'. This was the only spectre at the feast – a spectre whose features were those of Napoleon I . . . Victoria and Albert were lodged at Saint-Cloud in Marie-Antoinette's apartments; they went over the Exhibition and the Palais des Beaux Art: picnicked at Versailles, visited the

Louvre, and danced at the Hôtel de Ville, and Victoria found Napoleon III 'quite charming, with such quiet amiability. He has the gift of attracting everyone who comes in contact with him'.

Paris, always quick to enthusiasm, was enchanted by the interlude at the Invalides. The Queen went there with the Emperor, Prince Albert, Prince Napoleon and Princess Mathilde. The work in the crypt, begun in 1843 and abandoned in 1848, was now in hand again, and the sarcophagus, covered with a purple pall embroidered with golden bees, rested in a side chapel. Veterans of the Empire carried torches to light up the scene, and while the visitors collected their thoughts a violent storm broke over the town. Victoria seemed to be deeply moved, and turning towards the little Prince of Wales, the future Edward VII, who looked charming in his Highland dress, she said:

'Kneel to the tomb of the great Napoleon.'

At this moment the organs blended the resonant notes of *God Save the Queen* with the din of the storm.

'Strange and marvellous,' said the enraptured sovereign. Napoleon had been displeased by Visconti's audacity in hollowing out the ground to make room for the regal crypt; he remarked to Victoria that it looked as if they were going to install 'a reservoir'.* She noted 'he is endowed with ... great *calmness* and even *gentleness*, and with a power of *fascination*, the effect of which upon those who became more intimately acquainted with him is most sensibly felt'.

The reconciliation did in fact seem complete. It was easy for Napoleon III to comply with many requests and raise the question of St. Helena.

* The Emperor's remains were put in place on April 2, 1861. Marchand, the sole survivor of the three executors, was made an officer of the Legion of Honour. Santini, former usher at Longwood was appointed guardian of the tomb.

Marchand survived the disaster of Sedan and only died in 1876, last French survivor of the exile on St. Helena.

X

ST. HELENA AGAIN

✳

Once Napoleon's body had embarked on *La Belle-Poule* St. Helena relapsed into the silence of its uneventful existence, but the English had great difficulty in obliterating the recollection of all that had happened on the theatre of the rock, and travellers insisted on going to meditate beside the empty tomb or in Longwood, tumbledown as it now was, and cluttered with cattle and poultry. The man who had suffered from Hudson Lowe's cruelty was too famous for the memory of his life in exile to be the concern of purely local history, and the hour of truth had been foretold by a poet – Heine once again: 'Until the remotest centuries the children of France will tell and re-tell the story of the terrible hospitality of the *Bellerophon*, and when those songs full of irony and tears echo across the water, the cheeks of all honest Englishmen will turn red.' When Napoleon used to amuse himself by hollowing out alleys and ponds or digging a conduit of water to his tiny reservoir, he made light of his unhappiness and predicted to the Grand Marshal with a trace of pride: 'When I am no longer here English travellers will sketch the garden Napoleon made. Every one of them will want to see it.'

The July Monarchy was living through its final days when two French naval officers, Captain Despointes of the frigate *l'Arminde*, and Captain Gatier of the *Reine-Blanche* put in at St. Helena and offered to buy the empty tomb, to save it from speculators. The governor of the colony was nonplussed; he objected that the transaction would have political repercussions, but said that he would pass on the offer to London, which had been duly filed along with the innumerable letters received deploring the desecration of Longwood. To come to a decision the backing of government and the resources of diplomacy were needed.

The details of the period of exile were as familiar to Napoleon III as was the map of the island which he had so often pored over with the former Betsy Balcombe: he knew the rough paths surrounding The Briars, the muddy plateau of Longwood, the long ochre and grey house, the silent valley where the spring flowed; he also carefully read all reports from navigators, which came to him annotated by the Ministry for Foreign Affairs. 'Would it not be desirable, Monseigneur,' wrote a certain M. de Saint-Maurice, harbour-master of Réunion, 'for France to buy this tomb, now empty of its sacred burden, and the surrounding huts which are being subjected to insult, and to fill up the former and reduce the latter to ashes, so that nothing should remain except the place itself, whose testimony will always be eloquent enough.'

Despite the indignation shown by the French visitors at the time of the ceremonies of 1840, nothing had been done to preserve these famous sites: the house was still used as a farm, and natives and cattle occupied its dirty, dilapidated rooms. People were getting so accustomed to this state of affairs that a complaisant governor had renewed the sordid lease to the farmer for another twenty-two years after it expired in 1850, even authorising the tenant to knock down part of the buildings in order to repair others ... At the site of the grave the same traffic in earth, water and fragments of masonry went on, and one had to pay three shillings for a look into the grave, all this to the great advantage of the honorary French consul, Solomon, who also carried on business as an innkeeper and hirer-out of carriages.

Guessing that the presence of 'Bonaparte's' nephew on the French throne might facilitate some profitable transaction, an associate of Solomon's laid claim in 1853 to Sane Valley, casually stating that he was acting on behalf of the Paris government ...

This affair created considerable agitation among the local

authorities, but the colonial judge foiled the plan by stating that foreigners could not own land in St. Helena. This legal argument still held good in Great Britain, and in 1854 Paris (having probably had underhand dealings with the individual in question) decided to make the transaction official and embark on diplomatic negotiations.

The French ambassador in London was none other than Count Alexandre Walewski, son of the Emperor and Marie Walewska, the man who should have been able to find the most convincing arguments. It is easy to imagine the astonishment of the Foreign Secretary when he saw this man with a high forehead and a striking resemblance to Napoleon entering his office, to talk to him in Napoleon III's name about the tomb on St. Helena. It was hardly possible to equivocate, and Walewski received 'a positive assurance that on condition that local legislation confirmed the order, the land in question could be registered in the name of any French subject, without the necessity of that French subject being naturalised at St. Helena (as had at first been believed)'.

Napoleon III gave orders that the deeds should be prepared in the name of Major Gauthier de Rougemont, a Waterloo veteran and protégé of the Grand Marshal of the Palace, Marshal Vaillant, that Longwood House should be included in the transaction, and that the new owner should take the title of custodian of the Emperor's house and tomb. Time passed, and two years later Walewski, now Minister for Foreign Affairs, dispatched his successor to London, emphasising that 'the procedure to be adopted, if only to counteract exaggerated pretensions ... was to ask the British Cabinet to have the said land bought by the governor of St. Helena'.* This dispatch was placed before the Foreign Secretary,

---

* Walewski's successor in London was Jean Fielin, Duc de Persigny. This former non-commissioned officer, attached to Napoleon III since 1835, had taken part in the attempted *coups* at Strasburg and Boulogne. Aide-de-camp to the Prince-President, he was also involved in the affair of December 2 in 'shutting in the Assembly'. He became ambassador in London in 1855, after having been Minister of the Interior from 1852 to 1854.

Lord Clarendon, and the Prime Minister, Lord Palmerston, who directed the Secretary of State for the Colonies to study the means, without delay, 'of realising the desire of the Emperor of the French'. They were confronted by the same difficulties as before: the greed of the owner of Napoleon Valley and of the tenant of Longwood House and the intransigence of the colonial judge, who believed the transaction to be illegal ... At the same time the two former individuals who were represented in Paris by a certain Monneron, had been discreetly treating with Napoleon ever since 1853, but could not guarantee possession of the property ... This was not for lack of gumption, for the intermediary had knocked at every door to obtain this assurance, even approaching the Prime Minister of the day, Lord John Russell, to whom he boldly wrote: 'We have sold the spot where the Emperor Napoleon was buried together with the house, about twenty-six acres, to the Emperor of the French. The inhabitants of the island are anxious that the whole property should become French property, so that the tomb of a man once so great should no longer be desecrated by the traffic made of it in allowing strangers to visit it on payment of three shillings.'

Letters and requests were sent to the governor of St. Helena, who referred them to his judge, only to be told the the law was categorical ... He remained stubborn until the day when a report from the Queen's Attorney General and Solicitor General was placed under his nose, which declared that the legislature of St. Helena was competent, by virtue of Acts 3 and 4 of the reign of William IV, chapter 85, paragraph 112, and of the Order in Council of 1834, to change the laws, and 'we therefore think that it would be lawful to pass an Ordinance, conferring on a foreign power to hold and transfer land within the colony of St. Helena'. It was of course necessary to satisfy the colony's Treasury whose situation was precarious and who were loth to lose the rent of Longwood: £2,000 was sufficient to remove the latter obstacle and it seemed as though the goal had been attained. In December 1856 the governor reported to his ministry the measures he had taken to realise the transaction: the proprietor of Sane Valley, a man called Pritchard, acting in co-operation with Monneron of Paris and Hudson Janisch (son of Lowe's former secretary) would be content with £1,600, and justified this fairly large claim by stating that the famous Barnum was among the would-be pur-chasers ... The threat of allowing the Val Napoleon and the tomb of the founder of his dynasty to fall into the hands of a circus proprietor was well designed to force the hand of the Emperor of the French ... The Longwood farmers claimed £3,500 or breach of his lease, and the colony £2,000 for the loss of the rent of the farm installed in Napoleon's apartments: this made a total of £7,000, or 175,000 francs. The purchase would be made with the help of funds from the British Treasury, repayment of which would be required from the French embassy in London after the transfer had taken place.

On March 18, 1858, governor Drummond-Hay at last promul-gated an Ordinance transferring 'to His Majesty the Emperor of the French and His heirs' Longwood House, and its adjoining land of about three acres, and the Val Napoleon with an area of thirty acres.

On April 29, 1857, Napoleon III signed the draft bill making available to the Minister for Foreign Affairs an extraordinary credit of 180,000 francs, 'destined for the acquisition of the tomb and dwelling-house of the Emperor Napoleon I at St. Helena'. The vice-president of the Council of State, M. de Parieu, and two councillors, M. Conti and M. Armand Lefebvre, were appointed to support the discussion before the Legislative Assembly and the Senate.

'Under a former government,' they recalled, 'the shore where Saint Louis expired in Tunis, near the ancient city of Carthage, was consecrated by a mausoleum. An equally splendid homage will be paid to the Emperor who died in the heat of the tropics. Thus two great memorials will stand at the two extremities of that African continent opened to civilisation by our arms. Scenes of glory have their own immortality, just as heroes do ... Marked out by a unique event, that little island of St. Helena is a historical monument in the middle of the ocean. Nothing can efface it from men's memories.' The session of May 11, 1857, gave deputy Edmond de Beauverger the chance to satisfy official lyricism: 'On May 5, 1821, Napoleon died, betrayed and slandered, almost alone, on the distant rock of St. Helena. His family were wandering and scattered; his work seemed to have been destroyed. Today the Bonaparte dynasty rules France again; the Empire, gloriously restored, promises the world a long period of peace. Nearly twenty years ago Paris greeted the return of the exile's remains with pious enthusiasm, and the dome of the Invalides received them ... There the last passions, the last hostile prejudices have gradually been laid to rest ... All sounds of discord die on the threshold of that sanctuary where only glory has its echoes. But the memory of the hero has not left St. Helena ... Navigators from all over the world stop at that rock, peopled by such amazing recollections. We must see that they find something more there than mere mercenary exploitation and unworthy desecration.'

The two hundred and thirty-one deputies present voted for the project and the senators did the same on May 29, and on June 6, 1857, Napoleon III signed the act of promulgation at Saint-Cloud.

On May 7, 1858, Queen Victoria presided over a private council attended by the Prince Consort, which ratified the Ordinance of the governor of St. Helena, and the French Ministry for Foreign Affairs repaid to the British Treasury the sum of 178,565 francs through the intermediacy of Rothschild's bank. This operation over, it became clear that the estates were not 'offered' to Napoleon III, as writers across the Channel soon began to say, but that the Queen had merely sanctioned this quite exceptional transaction, which consisted in handing over a patch of British soil to a foreign government or sovereign.*

* One cannot fail to notice that the estates were given to 'Napoleon III and his heirs', the term obviously referring to the Bonaparte family and not the French State. In any case the question is unimportant, since the ownership has never been

Major Gauthier de Rougemont, on his way to take possession of the domain with a missionary's faith and a veteran soldier's enthusiasm, had been in London since April to collect his credentials for St. Helena from the French ambassador. Alas! Persigny was packing for his return to Paris and the British Minister for the Colonies was in the country, as was also the first secretary of the embassy ... This was only the first disappointment in a mission which was to cause more than one wound to the brave old soldier's self-respect ... After forty-three days voyage in the 'servants' quarters below decks', he arrived at the Cape on May 18, accompanied by his wife, lady's-maid and batman, re-embarked on June 10 and arrived at the rock on the 30th.

On July 7, dressed in the uniform of an officer in charge of an imperial residence, he took possession of the domain, 'with deep, inexpressible emotion'. On August 15, full of curiosity, all the colonial officials attended a luncheon given by him in honour of Saint Napoleon, and the governor proposed the toast, standing in front of a portrait of Napoleon III and the Empress Eugénie: 'We are happy, my dear friend, that the Emperor should have chosen an officer of the Grande Armée to come here to look after and preserve the house and the tomb of the great Napoleon 1st.'* A good start had been made, but once the euphoria of this welcome had melted away he reluctantly realised that the work of repairing the ruins was beyond the powers of a retired cavalry officer, alone and short of means, and six thousand kilometres away from his administration ... The price of materials was prohibitive, one contractor named a sum of £3,500 to restore Longwood House alone, and officials, drilled to local difficulties, affirmed half-

---

* Gauthier de Rougemont was born in 1796. He entered the army in May 1811 at the age of fifteen. Present at forty campaigns, he was proud of the wound he received in 1813, of being mentioned in dispatches when in the army of Morea, and gaining ten other citations in Africa. His mother was lady-in-waiting to the Princess Borghese.

---

contested and by virtue of the Statute of Limitation cannot be contested any more.

seriously that if he employed native labour the major would not see the end of his undertaking for six years ... 'Local workmen are only useful to help the masons,' the custodian wrote at once to Paris, 'they don't even possess a plumb-line.' And he very intelligently suggested sending a senior officer in the engineers and a party of men. The result was that Captain Masselin, Mareschal and four sappers disembarked at Jamestown on March 1, 1869, and spent two years saving what could still be saved of Longwood House, as well as reconstructing the romantic decor of the Valley of the Tomb.

For lack of materials they had to pull down the pavilions where the Emperor's suite had lodged: the short thick grass which at once invaded the foundations was less shocking than the ruins of hen-houses and dovecots. Meanwhile precious relics were disappearing: Montholon's drawing-room, to which Napoleon often used to come to tease the languishing Comtesse, Gourgaud's room and those of the two Las Cases, the whole decor of the intimate dramas which explained so many episodes of the time of exile.

To help him restore the Emperor's own apartments Masselin had recourse to the memoir-writers of 1815, and scraped the walls in search of a fragment of wall-paper or flakes of paint; and soon the partitions were put up, floors were laid and woodwork moulded anew, while labourers dug the earth to find the exact plan of the gardens in 1821. Based on what they found, Masselin reconstructed the covered alley where Napoleon used sometimes to breakfast during the hot weather, just as we see it today.

At the same time the tomb was cleared, bricked up and re-covered with flag-stones cut on the spot, to replace those carried away on *La Belle-Poule*.* On July 20 it was finally closed and a lead plaque recalled the event:

* It is distressing to find that these stones were forgotten on *Le Belle-Poule*, stored in the arsenal at Cherbourg, and only found and brought to the Invalides in 1909.

H.M. Napoleon III, Emperor
M. Thouvenel, Minister for Foreign Affairs
the tomb of the Emperor Napoleon I
closed on May 9, 1821, opened on October 15, 1840
was once more closed on July 20, 1860, by Messieurs
    Gauthier de Rougemont, Major and custodian
    Masselin, captain of engineers
    Mareschal, guard of engineers
    Morilleau, sergeant 3rd regiment of engineers
    Margès, corporal 3rd regiment of engineers
    Moutardeau, master workman
    Brun, master workman

A deep trench, lined with dry stones, had been dug around the grave to divert the water infiltrating from the spring and ensure that the new masonry would resist the test of time. On December 20, 1859, a stone had been removed to be sent to the United States government, who wanted to embed it in the pedestal at the monument to Washington, erected in the federal capital: 'It would be a silent and solemn witness,' declared the American consul, 'to the importance of that friendship between two nations which began with our origins and has united us until the present day like a golden chain.'

The landscape, alas, had changed since 1821: twelve cypresses planted in about 1830 by Lady Dallas, wife of a governor, stifled the original willows, and as the domain was shut off from animals by a fence, the trees proliferated and transformed the valley into a forest.

In January 1861, before returning to France, Masselin handed over the restored estates to the Major: the work had cost 163,000 francs, and if the reconstitution was incomplete it had at least put a full-stop to the humiliating state of affairs. Sergeant Morilleau and Sapper Moutardeau, who were about to marry girls from the island, were respectively appointed guardians of Longwood and the Tomb with salaries of 4,000 and 3,000 francs a year. They wore uniform when receiving visitors, who were numerous at the time because the Suez Canal was not yet in use. The Major was installed at New Longwood, never occupied by Napoleon, and only wore his uniform of officer of imperial residences to receive people of importance, such as Queen Victoria's son, Prince Alfred, or Admiral Sir Charles Elliot, appointed governor of the colony in 1863. When making his formal visit on arrival, the latter drew the Major aside to a corner of the park, suddenly stopped and said:

'It was here, in 1819 or 1820, when I was midshipman on a passing vessel, that I saw your Emperor walking in his little garden.'

French sailors and soldiers returning from China used to climb the dusty road behind their officer, and gather round the stone while the Waterloo veteran told them about the man who had led their fathers to victory: 'Look well at everything around you, so that you can tell them at home that someone who had all the kings of Europe at his feet lay for twenty years under a grass-covered grave.'

On September 13, 1861, the Abbé Coinde, chaplain of the battleship *La Saône*, commanded by Lieutenant Collos and returning from Cochin China and Réunion, blessed the re-closed tomb and the restored house in the presence of one hundred and fifty men of the navy and marines. In August the custodian had sent the original fence that had enclosed the tomb, as well as the leaden basin from Longwood gardens, to the harbour-master at Brest, to be forwarded to Napoleon III.

After nine years on the island, the old officer started home to take the waters in France in 1867, but he was destined never to return to the plateau of Longwood where enthusiasm and faith had supported him and kept him company. He found Paris caught up in the whirl of the second Universal Exhibition: sovereigns were cantering beside Napoleon III, among them William of Prussia, future conqueror of Sedan, and the capital was given over to official festivities. Soon afterwards came the opening of the

Suez Canal, but all the chancelleries of Europe knew that the star
of Empire was waning, for there were menacing clouds hanging
over the Rhine, and by becoming a liberal to meet the nation's
wishes the Emperor was only hastening to meet his doom. In
November 1868 while an unknown young barrister called
Gambetta was defending the editor of *Réveil* against the charge of
opening a subscription for a monument in memory of Baudin,
who had died on the barricades in December 1851, he launched a
violent attack on the régime in open court: 'On December 2, men
as yet unknown to France, and possessing neither talent, honour,
rank nor position, stood grouped round a pretender. One might
say of those men what Sallust said of the rabble surrounding
Catiline.' A few months more, and Thiers would declare at the
tribune of the Legislative Assembly: 'There is no fault left
uncommitted.'

How could this ill, ageing Emperor avoid committing them?
His Waterloo was to be called Sedan.

*   *   *

The *coup d'état* of December 2 had quite naturally stimulated
the anger of the anti-Bonapartists, whose aim had been to attack
the régime in the person of the founder of the dynasty.

Jules Barni, 'martyr to free thought' and an exile in Switzerland, had written *Napoleon and his historian M. Thiers*, with the
intention of destroying both the writer (whom he thought
devoid of all moral sense) and Napoleon, who had dammed the
course of the Revolution, who 'scorned humanity, despised other
people's opinion, was as proud as Caesar, unfeeling, indifferent
to morality – all faults which prove that Napoleon was not funda-
mentally French'.

D'Haussonville, married to the granddaughter of Madame de
Staël (whom Heine wittily described as 'a Robespierre in petti-
coats'), and a fervent catholic and liberal of Lamennais' school,
had attacked the Empire's religious policy, but received a snub

from the Vatican, whose archivist Father Theiner, had written an apology for the Concordat and its initiator.

Edgar Quinet had also gone to ground in Switzerland ... To this enemy of religion, who thought of the Church as an obstacle to social progress, the Revolution constituted a stage towards a nobler and more humane world, and Napoleon was merely a military genius who had used his capital of glory to attain base political ends, the enemy of civil power and the champion of brute force: this conqueror who aspired to be an Emperor like Constantine or Theodosius had nothing French about him – he was entirely Italian.

Pierre Lanfrey, journalist, politician and historian, tried to erase the entire legend and deflate the balloon of the Third Empire – a task which failed to rescue him from literary obscurity.

Then came Michelet ... Three volumes on the Directory, the Consulate and the Empire appeared in 1872 and 1873. This fanatical admirer of the Revolution and its message of civilisation used all his talent to attack the popular idol, the 'tuppence-coloured' print of the Little Corporal: the vulgarity of his character, victories due to chance rather than science, cowardice at the time of 18 Brumaire, unhealthy egoism – such was the conqueror who must be asked the terrible question: 'What have you done to France?' The English had been wrong – a hundred times wrong – to send him to St. Helena, where he had inspired pity while hatching fresh lies to carry him back to the bloody follies of imperial power. Was the historian of the First Empire perhaps chewing over the grievances of a professor who had been suspended and then dismissed by the Second? One is tempted to think so when Michelet affirms: 'I am still of the people,' thus siding with the man he exhausts himself to defame, that 'tyrant' who stormed in Roederer's presence: 'I am a soldier, a son of the Revolution, sprung from the people: I will not endure being insulted as a king.' Or was his claim to be a democrat overdone? What did it matter, Michelet's passion is as infectious as his ideas are liberal, and his style biting and vehement, and he easily communicated his strong impressions to his contemporaries.

In the 140 pages of *Origins of Contemporary France*, published in 1890, Taine drew a terrifying portrait of Napoleon the *condottiere*: denuded of humanity, a fiend let loose, the victim of his passions like any other Italian – didn't he seduce his sisters like Borgia? – full of conventional ideas, egoistic and indifferent to law and public interest like all members of Corsican clans, hungry for conquests, indifferent to the fate of France ... The institutions he gave the country were in his own image: authoritarian, centralised, bureaucratic, and his University was planned merely to prepare young men to be sacrificed to the Empire. It was pressing positivism very far when he applied to a figure like Napoleon the magic formula: 'the genius of a man resembles a clock; it has its structure and all the pieces are connected by one great spring.' A spring that sets all the pieces in motion ... Yet Napoleon does not lend himself easily to theories of race, environment and opportunity: Taine could have put in their place sheer genius, vocation, and intensity of creative power. It must be said in his defence that his memory was so full of the humiliations of 1870 and the excesses of the Commune that he attacked the Revolution and the Empire with equally pessimistic bias, settling questions by deduction, condemning on abstract formulae and defending himself strenuously against any ideas that were so tiresome as to contradict his philosophy.

And then Bonapartism, believed to have died at Sedan, suddenly benefited from the misfortunes of the youthful Third Republic, the scandal of Panama and the Dreyfus Case, as is shown by the fact that in 1897 Maurice Barrès, in *Les déracinés*, sent a party of young men eager to serve their country on a pilgrimage to the Tomb in the Invalides. And the last of the opposition were only recruited among journalists and academics, who denounced with one voice a despotic militarism that no longer alarmed anyone. Among these was Emile Bourgeois, professor at the Sorbonne, who accused Bonaparte in his *Manual of foreign politics*, published in 1898, of being 'blinded by the mirage of the Orient', of having 'done violence to' history to give himself an occupation, of having made the people his tool and being responsible for wars and disasters. Such, too, was Edouard Driault, who decided that France had suffered from playing the part Napoleon had written for her; such were Aulard and Guérard, who rehashed Michelet's denunciations; or Pariset who imputed all responsibility for the Napoleonic wars to Bonaparte himself; or Jules Isaac, who spoke of 'blind despotism'; or Seignobos, who agreed with Driault; or finally Bainville, who turned the Emperor's life into a Greek tragedy, with its characters rushing inevitably to their doom – a warrior's version of the struggle of Jacob and the Angel.

In the opposite camp were famous names appealing to a more considerable audience: firstly, Henri Houssaye, whose two volumes, *1814* and *1815* gained him entrance to the Académie Française and were described by Anatole France as: 'Impartial history. No phrase-making, no empty or ornate words; truth to facts throughout, and the eloquence of things themselves.' Then Arthur Levy has given us *Napoléon intime* and *Napoléon et la paix* to disprove the thesis of an inhuman sovereign by refuting the evidence of such detractors as Madame de Staël and Madame de Rémusat, point by point. In 1894 Frederic Masson, an impassioned partisan but an honest and sincere historian, embarked on a series of books to which he devoted a quarter of a century. Albert Sorel, a cultivated and sensitive diplomat and professor at the School of Political Sciences and a brilliant stylist, gives his view of Napoleon as 'driven by the force of circumstances – in other words Europe, its rulers, its peoples, their claims, their traditions, their greed for more territory, their desires for supremacy'. Albert Vandal, an austere dialectician, presents Napoleon as the restorer of the greatness of the France of the Ancien Régime; his books describing the rise of Bonaparte explain with admirable clarity both his character and the reasons for his undertakings, while that on Napoleon and Alexander minutely analyses the causes of the Empire's downfall. All these writers opened the way for the modern school, such as Madelin, Aubry and Dunan, who justified popular admiration by scientific historical studies, based on the discovery of unpublished documents and the study of foreign archives.

XI

NAPOLEON REMEMBERED AT
ST. HELENA

❊

Sedan was already a date in French history when on the morning
of July 12, 1880, Sergeant Morilleau saw a little procession arriving in the valley of the Tomb, led by the governor, Hudson
Janisch, son of Lowe's former secretary. The lady in black whom
he was addressing so respectfully was none other than the Empress
Eugénie, on her way home from the Transvaal, after praying at
the place where her son had been massacred by Zulus. Her suite,
General and Lady Wood, Captains Slade and Bigge (friends of
Prince Louis), the Marquis of Bassano and Dr. Scott, stepped
tactfully aside when she approached the iron gate and remained
rapt in prayer with closed eyes before looking about her at the
austere landscape, apparently designed to surround the tomb of a
titan. She exchanged a few words with Morilleau and his wife,
and then went on to Longwood, whose empty rooms and tangled
garden seemed to her to have 'a melancholy beauty'. She asked
Janisch several questions about the legal status of the domains,
which she believed were the property of her family, and she smiled
when he told her that the terms of their cession to Napoleon III
'and his heirs', without reference to 'his successors' might be
understood to mean that they were possessed by the family rather
than the nation.

She took some refreshments at the pavilion of The Briars,
accepted an album of photographs of the island from the governor,
and gave audience to several ladies before returning to the mail-
boat *Trojan* on which she was a passenger. She had wanted to

visit St. Helena for a long time, she confided, 'but in the company of her unfortunate son.' She had come alone, alas, and doubly in mourning, to bring the homage of the Bonaparte family to this land of exile.

*   *   *

The Third Republic took over from the Empire at Longwood, but at very little cost. The honorary vice-consul, N. Solomon, grandson of the shopkeeper of Jamestown in 1815 and son of the witness to the return of the ashes, was charged with administering the property; Mareschal and Sergeant Morilleau successively received the title of guardian, the latter remaining at his post until his death in 1907. Mareschal was a veteran of the African and Roman campaigns. Born in 1835, Morilleau was seventy-two in 1907, and the father of twelve children. Like his master, Gauthier de Rougemont, he lived at New Longwood House, rented from the colonial government. Sapper Moutardeau died in 1873.

Lucien Morilleau was replaced by an agent of the Ministry for Foreign Affairs called Henri Roger, who remained at his post until 1917. His predecessor had been a conscientious quarter-master-sergeant, but was rather ignorant of the historical background, and the house presented an appalling spectacle. In 1885 the wall-papers put up by Masselin (copies of the originals) were replaced by others in dubious taste, and Roger had to scrape the walls and cover them again, in spite of which the rooms with their worm-eaten woodwork, broken shutters and stained textiles betrayed the ravages of time and the climate. 'It was rather like visiting a hunting-box to let,' wrote one traveller. 'All the doors were open. I wandered wherever I wished, trying to imagine what this house must have looked like but without success. In the first room, the one where Napoleon died, stands a little altar covered in blue, and opposite it the Emperor's bust. A wooden balustrade marks the spot where Napoleon breathed his last. All the other rooms are empty.'

It was now the turn of the English to frown at this dilapidation ... All the mail-boats from the Cape of Good Hope and quite a lot of vessels of the Royal Navy used St. Helena as a port of call, and this led to a great many visitors and a great many sharp comments. In 1910 Longwood and the Tomb were visited by the Duke of Connaught, brother of Edward VII, who wandered uneasily through the empty rooms and uncultivated gardens. At last in 1913 the historian Albéric Cahuet took up the scandal and made himself the advocate of a cause which was bound to find a response in France, now that it was free of the anti-Bonapartist politics that had been the heritage of Sedan. He was backed up by an Italian called Cavicchoni, who had recently been staying on the island; consequently, next year an extra sum of 20,000 francs was voted, and in 1914 Roger was able to start on the indispensable repairs, which were in fact to cost 30,000 francs. It was the beginning of a happier period, and thanks to the understanding of an administration anxious to maintain French prestige here as elsewhere, the estate little by little resumed its original aspect, and the Emperor's memory was honoured in simple but dignified surroundings.

Shortly after sending in a report of the work accomplished, Roger was recalled to France at his own request and for reasons of health, but his successor, George Colin, travelled to St. Helena on a vessel that was torpedoed in March 1917, and was unable to take over his duties until 1919, after a long stay in hospital. His wife lost the use of her legs as the result of the disaster, but courageously put up with the hard life of St. Helena. Colin's first impression was pretty disappointing. Longwood New House, the attractive building occupied by his predecessors, had been taken over by the government of the colony for the purposes of the Great War, and he and his family were obliged to lodge first in the tiny cottage in Geranium Valley, and afterwards in Longwood House itself, in what had been the Emperor's 'private apartments', namely two bedrooms, dining-room and library. Visitors could therefore only be admitted to the billiard-room and drawing-room.

After being shut for two years the building looked the worse for wear, and although the budget for upkeep had been raised from 3,000 to 6,000 francs a year, George Colin was forced to admit in 1920 that all he could undertake was a little painting.

On the eve of the celebrations of the centenary of the Emperor's death in 1921, he was however able to get some re-papering hastily done, so that those who collected in the drawing-room as dusk approached on May 5 did not have to blush for its décor. An euphoric atmosphere of Entente Cordiale had been revived by the War. Marshal Foch was president of the Centenary committee, and Gaston Chérau was at Longwood to represent French writers. There was a splendid ceremony at the Tomb, with a guard of honour provided by the British garrison, and Longwood House was lit up with a hundred candles. There was talk of 'the greatest genius who ever lived'. The cannon was fired the evening before and at every hour throughout the anniversary day. 'Who can be compared to Napoleon?' demanded the governor as he stood before the flagstone. 'The great conquerors of antiquity, Philip of Macedonia, Alexander the Great, Hannibal ... They were all imbued with the same desire, the same ambition to make their countries famous, and you will agree that that is a fine ambition for a patriot.'

Forgotten were Sir Hudson Lowe's tirades, the insulting caricatures of the last century, the ostracism of a whole school of historians! The commanding officer of the garrison placed a wreath on the stone in memory of the most famous representative of the profession of arms; then George Colin, deeply moved, declared that the glorious campaigns of 1854 and 1855, and of the Great War, had for ever dispelled the misunderstanding that had hung over the politics of the two nations, as it had hung over this empty tomb.

The new custodian lacked neither persistence nor knowledge, and at once settled down to various large undertakings in the shape of trenches, roofs, woodwork, drainage, for all of which he received substantial sums. Why this constant rebuilding, this interminable restoration? It may well be asked. The answer is to be found in a climate that ruins houses just as it corrodes ironwork, rots paper and destroys paint; in the termites – introduced into the island in 1860 – which immediately invaded Longwood plateau; in the bad situation of the house, fully exposed to the trade winds and built on clay soil which the first rains transform into a cesspool. Painting, repairs and removing the rust had to go on as continuously here as on a ship at sea.

The development of communications by sea between Great Britain and South Africa brought an increasing number of visitors to Longwood, and they often complained with reason of only being shown two rooms, and those empty. George Colin was far from comfortable in Napoleon's small rooms and was delighted to report these complaints, and suggest that Montholon and Gourgaud's apartments should be rebuilt, and the first abode of the Las Cases repaired, so that an office and workshops could be installed there.

A private organisation, the Society of the Friends of St. Helena, sponsored by Captain Lachouque, Mademoiselle de Las Cases and General Koechlin-Schwartz, undertook the expenses of the work in 1931 and generously paid a bill of 350,000 francs for its completion in 1934. The Emperor's rooms were opened to the public, dreadfully shabby it must be admitted, but more moving in their bareness than all the other imperial palaces. The British government had returned the billiard table, two globes, two consoles (one of them having been used as an altar during the exile) and a mirror; all of these came from the sale of 1821.

The house had barely regained its long low outline of 1821 when termites began to invade the woodwork, whether that of the original building, or of Masselin's restorations carried out in soft woods such as cedar or cypress, or of the latest rebuilding. All the framework attacked was replaced by cement, which had the unfortunate result of making the building dangerously heavy, and in spite of highly complicated anti-termite treatment, by 1945 there was talk of disaster rather than damage: the roofs were threatening to collapse, and visitors had to be refused admittance to the house.

It was still in this distressing condition when King George VI, Queen Elizabeth and their children arrived in 1947. Their astonishment reached the ears of the French ambassador in London, M. Massigli, who pleaded for further restoration. A French architect came out from Paris and recommended that all the woodwork should be replaced by material proofed against termites, which involved again dismantling the framework, doors, windows and floors. Two workmen were recruited in England and attacked this task under the supervision of the new consul, George Peugot: the work was to last six years, from 1950 to 1955, and cost nearly 30,000,000 francs, charged to the account of the Ministry for Foreign Affairs under the heading of upkeep of diplomatic and consular premises.

The results appear to be successful and the famous house has blossomed into a second youth, with its fresh colours only needing the patina of time, with teak woodwork and wall-papers copied from those of 1821. A reservoir was also made, so that the gardens could be kept up during the dry season. A few critical individuals have found the whole effect too visually pleasing, too green and flowery: they forget that in 1821 the building was extremely well kept up, the park luxuriant, flowers abundant (especially roses), and Noverraz's garden so well wooded that the light hardly penetrated it. The legend that Longwood was dark and dusty was hard to kill.

At the same time, out of the same grant, George Peugot rebuilt the cottage of the caretaker of the Tomb, making it an acceptable home for an islander at the bottom of that lonely valley, and also put up a fence all round the vast domain so as to keep out straying animals. In the calm thus restored every passer-by must be assailed by memories of the past: on May 9, 1821, a cannon had thundered but it was English; flags fluttered in the wind, but they were embroidered with the names of the Empire's defeats in Spain; and the soldiers who carried the body of the last conqueror and the most famous prisoner in history on their shoulders wore the red coats of the victors of Waterloo. The French wanted to have 'Napoleon' engraved on the tombstone; Hudson Lowe had insisted on 'Napoleon Bonaparte'. The governor won this contemptible final victory and the stone remained bare. It still is. A few steps away, hidden among the arums and moon lilies, tiny frogs croak beside the spring whence, from 1815 to 1821, water was fetched for an imperial table, reduced to the status of a garrison mess. The willows have disappeared long ago, mutilated by souvenir-hunters, and their leaves dispersed by the wind of legend to the four corners of the globe; cypresses were planted in their place by Lady Dallas (in 1830); an olive by the Prince of Wales (future Duke of Windsor); a wild olive by Prince Philip, Duke of Edinburgh – and three monkey-puzzles by the crew of the *Jeanne d'Arc* in 1935, 1958 and 1963. All these grew in the shade of three gigantic Norfolk Island pines, planted by Masselin in 1860. This training-ship of the French navy has the honour to remember regularly that the exile of St. Helena was the legitimate sovereign of France. The white uniforms of the cadets and crew, standing in a circle around the flagstone make a brilliant patch in the green decor; the chaplain recites the prayers for the dead; bugles sound; the *Marseillasie* rings out and then silence returns once more – a silence suitable to the ashes 'which weighed on the world'.

Some of the original furniture has been put back in Longwood House, and copies have replaced those pieces that were missing: if the Emperor were suddenly to return from a drive in his calash he would recognise the table on which his valet used to put his gloves, field-glasses and snuff-box, the sofa in front of the fire where he spent so many sad hours, and the copper bath made by the sailors of the *Northumberland*. Marchand would only have to rearrange the pieces on the chess-board before going to prepare his camp-bed for the night, while Gourgaud might have given himself airs by looking at his Commission as a member of the Legion of Honour, now a museum piece shut in a glass case . . .

The ground in front of the house, excluded from the sale in 1858 for some unknown reason, was handed over by agreement with the British government in 1958, and the extension of the boundaries as far as the road running beside the house that once belonged to the Bertrands gives the façade the appearance seen in Marchand's beautiful water-colour, now at Malmaison, which shows a well-planned park, verdant and full of flowers.

In the same year Dame Mabel Brookes, great-granddaughter of William Balcombe, bought the pavilion of The Briars, whose owners – Cables and Wireless – were threatening to destroy it, and offered it to France.* The fragile edifice has been repaired and restored, as have the adjoining rooms built in 1816 for the British admirals who were also guests of the Balcombes, and a charming museum has been installed, consecrated to the English witnesses of the exile, and the history of the island under the East India Company's control. Napoleon's room has been faithfully restored.

Many ghosts wander there: Betsy runs up the brick staircase to show the Emperor her pretty ball-dress trimmed with roses; the slight forms of Las Cases and his son venture arm-in-arm along the rough path leading to the waterfall, while, sitting on a low wall beside the acacia shading his tent, Gourgaud grumbles disapprovingly at the little girl's noisy intrusions . . . Was it one one of these witnesses who whispered, a few months ago, that we should get rid of the wild mango-tree which was hampering the growth of a young olive? When the roots were dug up, the remains of the goldfish pond came to light, beside which Napoleon used to dictate to Las Cases or play with Tom Pipe, Admiral Cockburn's Newfoundland dog – we had been looking for its site for a long time.

Among all consular and imperial residences, Longwood holds the record for length of occupation, for – except for the Tuileries – Napoleon only inhabited his palaces occasionally, when galloping

---

* This firm proposed to build a house for their director there, amalgamating in it the room the Emperor had occupied.

from Compiègne to Austerlitz, or from Fontainebleau to Schoen-brunn, whereas he spent six years in this unpretentious dwelling, more time than he had taken to conquer Europe. It is hardly surprising that his presence still survives there. One seems to hear his footsteps echoing on the drawing-room floor, and it is impossible to walk in the park without imagining the little group – the Emperor, Bertrand, Montholon, Madame de Montholon and Gourgaud, pacing up and down the sunken alleys, to be joined by Hudson Lowe and his secretary Major Gorrequer. It is only necessary to shut one's eyes and listen.

'Your conduct will bring reproaches on your nation and your government ... You are always talking about your instructions ... I have governed, and I know that there are missions and instructions which are only given to dishonourable men.'

The figure of the governor-gaoler disappears in the red glow of the sun as it sets behind the sinister fort of High Knoll.

The gardens are still swept by the same breeze that carried their words away one hundred and fifty years ago. On May 5, 1971, St. Helena celebrated the one hundred and fiftieth anniversary of the Emperor's death, by issuing two postage stamps, one representing the Tomb in Geranium Valley, whence the ghost of General Bonaparte seems to emerge and cross the Alps, after David's picture; the other Napoleon by Delaroche.

The French government was represented at the official ceremonies by the Ambassador Etienne de Crouy-Chanel, whose flag was hoisted on board *Le Frondeur*. He declared: 'Although our era has questioned so many accepted beliefs, it has not seriously attacked Napoleonic values, so certain is it that the facts of his life are beyond question, and that the imperial achievement remains extraordinarily real and alive, even in these days of scepticism.' The British governor, Sir Dermod Murphy replied: 'The man in the street knows, and we are reminded by our education, that we are celebrating the memory of greatness, genius and courage.'

'How everything in this world changes!' as Chateaubriand would have said.

SELECT BIBLIOGRAPHY

❋

Antommarchi (Dr.) – *Les derniers moments de Napoléon.*

Apponyi (comte) – *Ving-cinq ans à Paris.*

Bainville (J.) – *Napoléon.*

Barni (J.) – *Napoléon et son historian, M. Thiers.*

Barrès (M.) – *Les déracinés.*

Bertaut (J.) – *Le faubourg St. Germain sous la Restauration.*

Bignon (L.) – *Histoire de France depuis le 18-Brumaire jusqu'en 1812.*

Boigne (Comtesse de) – *Mémoires.*

Bonaparte (Joseph) – *Lettres d'exil.*

Bourgeois (E.) – *Manuel de politique étrangère.*

Bourgoing (J. de) – *Le fils de Napoléon.*

Bourrienne (L.) – *Mémoires.*

Cahuet (A.) – *Après la mort de l'Empereur-Retour de Sainte-Hélène.*

Charles-Roux (F.) – *Rome, asile des Bonapartes.*

Chateaubriand (A. de) – *Mémoires d'Outre-Tombe.*

Chéreau (G.) – *A Sainte-Hélène* (Illustration, 25th June 1921) *Sainte-Hélène aujourd'hui* (Illustration, 2nd and 9th July 1921).

Coquereau (Abbé) – *Souvenirs du voyage à Sainte-Hélène.*

Dansette (A.) – *Louis-Napoléon à la conquête du pouvoir.*

Déchamps (J.) – *Sur la légende de Napoléon.*

Driault (E.) – *La vraie figure de Napoléon.*

Forsyth (W.) – *History of the captivity of Napoleon at St. Helena from the letters and journals of the late Lt.-General Sir Hudson Lowe.*

Gonnard (Ph.) – *Les origines de la légende napoléonienne.*

Guizot (F.) – *Mémoires pour servir à l'usage de mon temps.*

Haussonville (d') – *L'Eglise romaine et le Premier Empire.*

Hauterive (E. d') – *Sainte-Hélène au temps de Napoléon et aujoird'hui.*

Hazlitt (W.) – *Life of Napoleon Bonaparte.*

Heine (H.) – *Reisebilder: De la France.*

Hobhouse J. C., Lord Broughton – *Recollections of a long life.*

Houssaye (H.) – '*1814*'–'*1815*'–*Napoléon homme de guerre.*

Hugo (V.) – *Choses vues* (1ère série) *Le retour de l'Empereur.*

Isaac (J.) – *Cours complet d'histoire.*

Jackson (E.L.) – *St. Helena.*

Joinville (Prince de) – *Vieux Souvenirs.*

Karr (A.) – *Les Guêpes.*

La Gorce (P. de) – *Louis-Philippe.*

Landor (W.S.) – *The complete works.*

Lanfrey (P.) – *Histoire de Napoléon 1er.*

Langé (F.) – *Funérailles de l'Empereur Napoléon.*

Las Cases (Comte de) – *Mémorial de Sainte-Hélène.*

Las Cases (Emmanuel de) – *Journal écrit à bord de la frégate La Belle-Poule.*

Lefebvre (A.) – *Histoire des Cabinets de l'Europe pendant le Consulat et l'Empire*

Lévy (A.) – *Napoléon intime. Napoléon et la paix.*

Lieven (Princesse de) – *Correspondance.*

Lucas-Bubreton (J.) – *Le culte de Napoléon.*

Masson (F.) – *Napoléon inconnu. Napoléon et sa famille. Napoléon à Sainte-Hélène.*

Mazuyer (V.) – *Mémoires.*

Metternich (Prince de) – *Mémoires, documents et écrits divers.*

Michelet (J.) – *Histoire du 19ème siècle.*

Millanvoy (L.) – *Seconde vie de Napoléon.*

Musset (A.) de – *Confession d'un enfant du siècle.*

Napoléon (Prince) – *Napoléon et ses détracteurs.*

Pasquier (Chancelier) – *Histoire de mon temps.*

Planat de la Faye (L.) – *Rome et Sainte-Hélène de 1815 à 1821.*

Quinet (E.) – *Histoire de la campagne de 1815.*

Rose (J. H.) – *The life of Napoleon. The personality of Napoleon. Napoleonic studies.*

Rosebery (Lord) – *Napoleon, the last phase.*

Runciman (Sir Walter) – *The tragedy of St. Helena.*

Sorel (A.) – *L'Europe et la Révolution française.*

Stendhal – *Napoléon. Journal de Londres. Vie d'Henri Brulard.*

Taine (H.) – *Les origines de la France contemporaine.*

Thackeray (W.) – *The second funeral of Napoleon.*

Thiers (A.) – *Histoire du Consulat et de l'Empire.*

Touchard (J.) – *La gloire de Béranger.*

Vandal (A.) – *L'avènement de Bonaparte. Napoléon et Alexandre 1er.*

Vaulabelle (A. de) – *Histoire des deux restaurations.*
Veauce (Baron de) – *L'affaire du masque de Napoléon.*
Viennete (J.) – *Journal.*
Vigny (A. de) – *Servitude et grandeur militaires.*

Archives: *Archives of French Domains, St. Helena. Archives of the Government of St. Helena. Archives of the French Foreign Ministry.*

INDEX

❈